The Revealed Rome Handbook 2017/18

ISBN: 9781521068465

Table of Contents

Chapter 1
Getting Started

Welcome to Rome – and to Revealed Rome

Few cities in the world are as fascinating, complex, multi-layered, or downright beautiful as Rome. There's something to explore, and experience, in every corner.

In many ways, there is no better time to go to Rome than now. The Trevi Fountain has been restored to its former gleam; the Colosseum is clean for the first time in centuries. Small green spaces and new access areas to ancient ruins have sprung up across the capital, from the landscaping around the Temple of Hercules Victor to the walkway across the Imperial Forums. The restaurant scene is getting a shakeup with Michelin-starred restaurants and new chefs. Once-gritty areas are becoming vibrant with urban art, nightlife and music. After its success with Palazzo Valentini, the city is experimenting with other 21st-century approaches to ancient ruins, including light shows that bring the Imperial Forum to life and a new virtual reality-augmented tour of the Domus Aurea.

But all of that means the capital is popular as never before –

and just as full of pitfalls for tourists. For every step forward, there's a step back: The tourist charged €50 for an ice cream at a cafe, the cab drivers who refuse to take you for the legal fare from Ciampino into Rome, the globalization pushing small artisans and family-run shops out of business. That's not to mention the sheer crowds, which seem to get exponentially bigger every year.

Rome remains an extraordinary, vibrant city, and no matter how many visitors come, at heart, it still remains the same: A place that is in many ways more town than city, where to get the most out of it, you need to know it like an insider – or have the advice from one. That's where I can help.

I don't just mean tips to help you experience, in the most rewarding way possible, the famous sights like the Colosseum and the Sistine Chapel. I also mean knowing about the city's hidden secrets, whether that's an artisan selling handcrafted leather goods, a tiny church with glittering 9th-century mosaics, or a hole-in-the-wall *trattoria* filled with the bustle of Romans and the smell of *amatriciana*. These finds are everywhere – and they're what make Rome one of the best-loved (and most-visited) cities in Europe, if not the world. These kinds of gems aren't always that apparent to the short-term visitor. Some of the local spots and secrets I've included in this book took me years to find (or figure out).

Equally baffling can be how to do Rome as the locals do. What does it mean to "validate" a bus ticket (and why is it important)? Why shouldn't you shop between noon and 4pm? Where do you find bathrooms while out and about? How do you order a coffee with milk (and no, it isn't called a "latte")? What should you know to avoid being taken advantage of by scam artists, pickpockets and taxi drivers? How can you skip the lines? To understand and enjoy Rome, a city that foreigners can find as frustrating as it is fascinating, these tricks are just as important as the hidden gems.

Why should you take my word on any of this? A journalist and BBC editor, I'm the blogger behind the popular website Revealed Rome (revealedrome.com), which features tips and tricks to the Eternal City. I spent more than four years not only living in Rome, but making a career out of exploring and writing about it every single day: I have written dozens of travel stories on Rome and Italy for publications including the *BBC, National Geographic Traveler, New York Times, Globe & Mail, Travel & Leisure, New York Magazine, Travel Channel* and more; contributed to the Rome, Italy and Europe editions of numerous Fodor's guidebooks; and appeared in videos online and on television for the BBC, History Channel and (in an upcoming project) Netflix, speaking about Rome and Roman history.

Rome still feels like home to me today. It's a city I not only continue to visit several times a year, but which remains a major part of my livelihood, my friendships – and my spirit. If you've already visited, you probably understand why: This is not a city that will let you go. And if you are planning your first visit, please accept my envy. There is nothing like discovering for the first time why, exactly, people from around the world find this city so compelling, so seductive, and so difficult to leave.

How Rome – and this book – have changed

I published the first edition of this e-book back in 2012. While Rome changes more slowly than many other cities, it's fair to say that now, five years later, not everything is exactly the same. Back then, Berlusconi just had left office, Rome's third metro line seemed forever stuck in its archaeological-excavation phase and people thought that the €25 million Colosseum restoration might be too controversial because of its private funding. Now, Italy has cycled through two more prime ministers, almost half of Line C is up and running and private funding has not only cleaned up the Colosseum, but gone on to restore the Trevi Fountain, Spanish Steps and Rome's Pyramid. Even in Rome, things change.

On a personal note, I've also discovered a great deal more about the city, and – not least from talking to more than 250 clients in my travel consulting sessions over the years – learned more about what visitors to Rome really want to know, whether they're coming to the city for the first time or the fifth.

As a result, this is more than an update of information and

advice (although there's that, too). It's an expansion. I've added sections on everything from how to decide if you need a Roma Pass to why you should never take a taxi from Ciampino airport, from how to eat well with dietary restrictions to how to approach organizing your sightseeing, from how much Italian you should plan to speak to the best ways to get data and wifi on your phone or tablet. In fact, this book is twice the length of the original version. But I've kept the structure as easy to navigate and digest as it was before, dividing the information up not geographically, but in the way that seems more useful to travelers: By stage of planning. (More on what that means, and how best to use this book as a tool, next).

How to use this book

By the time you've found this book (or my website), you're probably already juggling a lot of information: Flight and hotel itineraries, various guidebooks, and recommendations from friends and travel agents. You may be feeling a little overwhelmed.

This book's purpose is to make things easier.

For one, it is important to know that – while there are sections where I share some of my favorite off-the-beaten-path sights, good-value hotels, authentic restaurants and artisanal shops – this is not a standard guidebook. There are any number of books and websites where you can find information about, for example, the Colosseum's history, location, hours and ticket prices. Instead of providing information easily found elsewhere, this book instead gives you tips and tricks for experiencing the Colosseum (and everything else) like a true insider – including how to skip the line, why you should ignore the tour guides hustling you outside, what else is nearby that you might want to do in the same chunk of time and alternative ways to experience the site.

This book also is organized a little differently than you might expect. Because it isn't meant to be an encyclopedic list of places and sights, for example, it isn't organized by neighborhood.

Instead, it's structured in terms of the steps most of us take when we're planning a trip, starting with what to know, think about and plan for before (or as) you make your very first bookings and ending with information you easily could read once you're already there. Part of the benefit of this is that, particularly if you're feeling a little overwhelmed, you don't have to feel like you have to sit down and read the whole book, cover-to-cover, right this second. Instead, you can use the book and use different sections as you plan, leave for, and enjoy your trip. Another benefit is that you're less likely to miss out: This structure makes it clear which sights, restaurants and other activities you need to book in advance, for example, so that you don't arrive in Rome and find it's too late.

As early as possible once you've decided on Rome as your destination, I'd recommend starting with "Before You Go: Planning, Booking, and a Little More Planning." This covers what you must do before you leave, like figuring out when to come to Rome (and how long to come for), reserving (and saving money on) your flight (or train ticket) and hotel, booking certain activities and restaurants in advance, and figuring out what to pack. This is also where I address some questions that tend to come up at the start, like whether you need to speak Italian, whether you should take any tours, if the Roma Pass makes sense to buy and whether you should rent a car. Even if you already have your dates, hotel, and flight covered, give this a skim, as there are likely to be some topics you may not have considered.

The next section can be read just a couple of days in advance of your trip. This chapter, "En Route to Rome: Transport and Logistics," covers how you'll get around the city – including how to get from the airport to your hotel, how to take a taxi (without getting ripped off) and how to take public transportation (as well as where to buy tickets for the bus, tram and metro). You can read this section before you leave (you may want to refresh yourself on it when you're on your flight), but you don't necessarily have to read it months in advance.

The same goes for "En Route to Rome: Graffiti and Crime." If you're concerned about safety and scams in Rome and want to know if, say, you should buy a money belt in advance, it can be worth reading ahead of your trip. Otherwise, you can leave it till later – even your flight over.

When you read the final three sections – "When in Rome: Sightseeing," "When in Rome: Eating," and "When in Rome: Shopping" – is, of course, up to you. If you're a planner and want to decide in advance which sights to see, how to schedule your itinerary, how to find good food, where to shop, and so on, then read these sections before you leave. If you're more the let's-see-how-it-goes-and-just-explore type, then these sections can be read anytime – on the plane, in your hotel room at night as new questions occur to you, or even on the go.

Again, for more tips and tricks, check out the Revealed Rome website. If you still have burning questions about your trip or want to receive personalized advice, I also offer one-on-one Italy travel chats over FaceTime, Skype or Google Hangout, giving you the chance to pick my brain about anything regarding travel in Rome and around Italy. Since launching this service in 2012, I've helped more than 250 clients plan their trips – including couples enjoying honeymoons or 30th wedding anniversaries, families with small children, young women traveling alone and teachers taking groups of students. (Over the five years I've provided this service, some of my clients even have planned second trips to Italy... and booked me again for more advice!). But I think it's safe to say that I've included so much in this update, 90% of readers will find this provides them with more than enough tips, tricks and, not least of all, confidence that the book alone will be enough to plan a fun, rewarding trip to Rome.

Happy trip planning, and no matter what, enjoy your time in the Eternal City!

Chapter 2
Before You Go

Planning, Booking (and a Little More Planning)

Even the most free-spirited travelers among us need to book flights and hotels... as well as, obviously, decide what time of year to travel, how long to stay for, and which sights and activities to book in advance. So this section isn't just for the super-planners. Instead, everyone visiting Rome should try to read it as far in advance of their trip as possible.

This chapter covers:

•scheduling your trip to Rome (including what to expect in each season and how much time you should spend in Rome versus other destinations)

•tips for booking flights, and the differences between Rome's two airports

•if you're arriving to Rome from another city in Italy, how to book train tickets

•the benefits and drawbacks of various types of

accommodation – from Airbnb to hotels to convents

•how to pick a neighborhood for your stay

•sights that you should book in advance to avoid waiting in line (plus sights that you must book in advance in order to enter at all)

•whether to buy a Roma Pass, one of its competitors… or none of the above

•how to decide whether to take a tour and if so, which type and where

•other common questions, including how much Italian you'll be expected to speak and whether to rent a car

•two last things you may want to consider booking in advance: some restaurants, and a private transfer from the airport (maybe)

•a couple of last items to take care of before you leave to ensure you can get internet, phone calls and money while abroad

•some tips for what to wear in Italy

•items to pack you may not have considered

•and finally, tips, tricks and recommendations to help you mentally prepare – and get excited! – for your trip to Rome.

When to come to the Eternal City

Fact: Rome is beautiful year-round. But depending on your preferences – and your availability – you might find you fall in love a little bit more some times of year than others. Before you pull the trigger on booking those flights (or on asking your boss for days off), here are some things to take into account.

Rome in the summer

Ah, summer. It's the time of year when you'll get a tan just by walking the cobblestoned streets; when prosecco on the *terrazza* of your Airbnb feels like as much of a must-do as seeing the Sistine Chapel; when gelato is a right, not a privilege.

Less poetically, it's also when the kids are out of school and office life (might) slow down, making it an easier time of year to get away. So it makes sense that you might be considering coming to Rome in those sunny, halcyon months.

Just remember: Everyone else is thinking the same way that you are. As a result, this is also the season when the hotels are full (and at their peak prices), the Colosseum is packed, and you have to stand on tiptoe to get a look at the Vatican's Laocoön. Not to mention that it's hot and sweaty... and many Italians don't believe in air-conditioning. (That includes at the Vatican museums, by the way).

How hot does it get, you ask? In July, when average temperatures peak, you're looking at an average high of 88°F (31°C); it remains almost as hot throughout August. (If you're looking at average temperatures online, don't be fooled: Although the average low is a comfortable 62°F (17°C), unless you're planning on staying out all night, it's guaranteed that you'll sleep through that respite). July is also the driest month of the year, with less than an inch of average rainfall. If you can swing it, June is milder and less crowded than either July or August, particularly earlier in the month.

"Oh!", you say, "but I love the heat and the sun! This isn't a problem for me!" That may be true, but keep in mind that 90°F (32°C) weather is one thing when you're experiencing it in on short walks between your air-conditioned office, house and car. It can feel very different when you're walking around all day (or trying to stuff yourself onto crowded, sweaty buses and trains)... visiting sites with little to no shade... when many restaurants, apartments and even museums lack air-conditioning.

In terms of crowds, going earlier or later in the summer can help, but not significantly. High season really kicks off in April in Rome, gets into serious high gear in June, and doesn't abate until October. When it comes to the crowds, June *definitely* counts as the summer. So does September. (Still, those months remain slightly better than July or August).

If you have to visit in the summer, then do try at least not to come to Rome between mid-August and mid-September. That's because *ferragosto*, the ancient (and beloved) Italian holiday, starts on August 15. Although it's supposed to be for just a couple of weeks, many families extend it into September. This used to mean that nearly all of Rome's family-run shops and restaurants shuttered up. While the city's increasing cosmopolitanism (or the struggling economy, take your pick) have meant that more local spots are remaining open for more of *ferragosto* than in the past, it's still a relatively tricky time of year and one I would recommend trying to avoid.

Rome in the autumn

First, let's be clear about one thing: In terms of heat and crowds, September is summer in Rome. (It even has the same average temperature as June, with highs of 82°F/28°C). So by autumn, I specifically mean October or November.

I can't recommend coming to Rome in those months more highly. When I moved to Rome in October, it was described to me by a local as a "magic month". He couldn't have been closer to the truth. The days are balmy, but the nights slightly crisp. When the trees change color, they make a city that's already a panorama of pinks and oranges and yellows even more colorful. Even the light feels different, more golden and, yes, magical.

Here's what the weather in Rome is typically like for most of the fall: mild (think highs of 73°F/23°C in October, getting down to 62°F/17°C in November), often with clear, sunny days and chilly nights. However, you do run a risk of rain. In fact, November tends to be the wettest month Rome sees year-round. And it can, indeed, be rainy. On average, Rome in November gets twice as much rain as London (!), and a smidge more than Boston or New York City. But the difference is that usually – *usually* – when it rains in Rome, it pours down... then stops. Yes, it might pour down again a couple of hours later. And it can be near-torrential – hence that high average. But it doesn't tend to be the week-long drizzle that you get elsewhere.

Weather aside, the benefit of October or November is that, of course, the crowds are much less than you'd get in the summer. There can still be a surprising number of people at some sites, particularly through October, but it doesn't compare to what you see in June or July. Prices reflect this. You're not going to find bargain-basement hotel prices in October, but you'll be paying far less for flights and accommodation (albeit more than in November, January or February) than you would in the summer.

Rome in the winter

If you're not a heat-and-crowds person, this is your season! (Outside of Christmas and New Year's week, that is). In December, January and February, there's an average high of about 55°F (13°C); it can get as low as 35°F (2°C) but, again, you're probably sleeping through this (and this time, that's probably a good thing). While you're out and about, plan for it to be generally around 45°F, or a little under 10°C.

While that's a bit chilly for some, the upside is it also tends to be drier and sunnier than the fall: For the most part, crisp and clear is the name of the game. Even so, December, January and February remain wetter than March, April and May, on average.

If you're willing to bundle up and bring an umbrella, the benefits of coming in the winter are many. For one thing, the crowds are at their lowest. So are the fees. It's not uncommon for a boutique hotel or upmarket B&B to halve their room prices in early December, late January or February because of the relative lack of demand. The same, of course, goes for airfares.

If you're coming over Christmas and New Year's, though, it's a different situation. In some ways, it's an even better one. Rome sparkles this time of year; the cobblestoned streets of the historic center are strung with stunning lights from early December until early January, the shop windows are bursting with beautiful, beribboned displays, and several Christmas markets take place in the city (though these aren't as many, or as elaborate, as you might expect: Christmas markets remain a more northern European tradition than they are a Mediterranean one). Of course, if you're interested in seeing the Pope or attending a Christmas celebration at the Vatican, so much the better. That being said, this is also a mini-high season in what is otherwise a low season – so if you want to come over Christmas or New Year's, be prepared for more people and higher prices than if you came a week earlier or later.

Rome in the spring

Another beautiful season. The flowers are blooming, people are gathering in the piazzas and there's green where you least expect it... even cascading down buildings in the form of ivy. Like autumn, spring is another "shoulder season" for tourism in Rome, particularly before Easter, so you're looking at lower (but not rock-bottom) prices and smaller (but not nonexistent) crowds. (Again, that doesn't apply to Easter week, which – like Christmas and New Year's – is a high-season situation, with prices and crowds to match).

If you'd like to experience spring at its warmest and sunniest, aim for May. That's often when my first beach days of the year have been, since the month sees an average temperature of 75°F (24°C), getting hotter toward the end (obviously), with about 1.5 inches (almost 4cm) of rain on average – roughly the same as August. March and April are much more mild, as well as wet: April is a very comfortable 67°F (19°C), but also sees an average of almost an inch more rain than May; March, which is as rainy as April, tops out at an average high of 61°F (16°C).

How much time to spend in Rome

The classic Italy itinerary is a week or 10 days long and hits Venice, Florence, and Rome. Ambitious travelers might wedge Pompeii, the Amalfi coast or a day in Tuscany in there, too.

I completely understand the temptation to follow this kind of schedule, particularly for first-time visitors. No matter where you've come from, getting here is expensive, traveling is a privilege, and if you're not sure when (or if) you'll get to come back, you want to make sure you're not "missing" anything.

Before you structure your trip in that way, though, do consider the major flaw in that argument: No matter how many cities you hit on that week-long itinerary, you'll always "miss" something. I have spent years of my life, quite literally, traveling around and experiencing Italy. Yet there are still many places and sights –

whole cities, even – that I've "missed". That's what makes Italy such a rewarding destination: It's overwhelmingly, excitingly rich with things to do, see, and experience.

As a result, although everyone travels differently, I'd think about shifting your mindset. You're going to miss things. That's a fact. But for the things you do get to see, would you rather be rushing through them, stressed about being ten minutes over schedule and missing the next item on the itinerary, worried about getting lost (which – unless you spend your whole trip glued to Google Maps on your phone – *will* happen) and seeing everything through the camera you're using to document you were there (even though you weren't even really 100% "there")? Or would you rather be *experiencing* what you're seeing – noticing the way the light slants through the oculus in the roof of the Pantheon, breathing in the smell of freshly-made espresso at a bustling cafe, looking at Bernini's Apollo and Daphne at the Borghese Museum until, maybe, they look so much like they've come to life, so full of emotion, you feel suddenly moved yourself? I know what I'd prefer, and I bet I know what you would, too. But it can be easy to forget that goal when you're making bookings online and finding how many fantastic sights there are you'd like to see – so every once in a while, make sure to check in with yourself (or your travel partner) and make sure that the itinerary you're designing really does reflect what you'd like to get out of your trip.

The other part that can be easy to forget, particularly if you come from an enormous country like the United States, Canada or Australia, is that even if destinations "look" close on a map, that doesn't mean they'll feel close once you're in Italy. Florence and Rome may be just three hours apart on the fast train. But that three hours doesn't include the time involved in traveling to and from the train stations, the buffer time you need to make your train, checking into your accommodation and getting re-oriented in another new place. Between your initial jet lag and these oft-forgotten time costs, a week (or even week and a half) doesn't leave you nearly as much time as you'd think – particularly if you're planning a "If it's Monday, it must be Venice"-type itinerary.

Meanwhile, even seeing *only* the major highlights of Rome takes at least two days. That's if you don't get lost or stuck in a long line, and it still excludes the vast majority of the city's sights and attractions, which may not be quite as famous as the Trevi Fountain but in many ways often are even more "worth" seeing.

So think carefully about exactly what you want your vacation to look like. If you want to do a day trip, or to have time to simply wander, or to sit and relax over a glass of wine, then don't pack your schedule. In four full days, you can have the time to balance both Rome's must-sees and a few of its other sites. But if you have five days or a week to spare, you'll enjoy the city even more (and give yourself the wiggle room for one or two day trips, if you want to get a taste of Italy beyond Rome).

If you take one thing away from this section, let it be this: When it comes to Rome, don't worry about running out of things to do. Instead, worry about how to plan so that you have the time you need to not only "see" the city, but to experience and enjoy it.

Booking flights to Rome

Once you've figured out when you're coming to Rome and how long you'll be here for, it's time to book your flight (assuming that's how you're arriving, of course).

If sticking to a budget is a priority, your airfare provides a good opportunity: Although flights can be expensive, there are many ways to save. Many general tips have been well-documented (e.g. book between Monday and Wednesday, join a frequent-flyer program, and ask for a refund if the fare drops after you bought it), so I won't spend too much time on those now.

Instead, I'll share some tricks that have worked for me specifically when I'm trying to book a round-trip flight to Rome from another country.

1) Consider European budget flights, but keep baggage (and your own sanity) in mind

If you're coming from outside of Europe, here's a trick to

getting to Rome cheaply: Find a (relatively) economical fare to London (or another hub – see below), and then hop on one of the many European budget airlines to get from there to Rome.

Originally just Ryanair (the yellow bus of the skies!) and EasyJet, the number of budget airlines in Europe have proliferated – so much that it's the rare savvy traveler indeed who thinks that taking a train around Europe is still the most budget way to go (though it does remain the most environmentally friendly). As of November 2017, budget airlines flying to Rome include (CIA to Rome Ciampino, FCO to Rome Fiumicino) :

- Vueling: from London, Paris, Stockholm, Dublin, Berlin and many others to Rome-FCO
- Ryanair: from Brussels, Lisbon, Madrid, London and many others to Rome-CIA or Rome-FCO
- EasyJet: from London, Paris, Geneva, Amsterdam and other European cities to Rome-FCO
- Wizz Air: flights from Bucharest, Prague and several eastern European cities to Rome-CIA
- Transavia Airlines: from Rotterdam only to Rome-FCO

Other airlines that fly to Rome but are not budget airlines (though they are worth checking, particularly as they often have sales and promotions) include Air Berlin, Alitalia and British Airways.

Within Europe, these flights can be extremely economical. On a recent search, I found flights in 2017 from Bucharest to Rome for €15 (at current exchange rates, $15/£12) with Wizz Air, London to Rome for €30 ($30/£25) with Vueling and Paris to Rome for €45 ($50/£40) with EasyJet. Note that some of these airlines do not come up when you search on an aggregator site like Google Flights or Expedia, so it's worth checking their sites individually.

Meanwhile, you can often find flights from the U.S. to European hubs like Dublin, London or Paris more cheaply than you can from the U.S. to Rome directly. To give you an idea, when I recently checked a random week for December 2017, a round-trip, nonstop flight from New York City to Rome was as low as $630. It was even less to fly from New York to London ($475) or to

Stockholm ($340). Combine a leg like that with a $30 flight, and you've gotten yourself to Rome for less than $400.

The trick is to be aware of what you're getting into – and of potential hidden charges. For budget airlines like Ryanair and EasyJet, these include fees for paying with a credit card or for needing to print the boarding pass at the airport, rather than having done so at home (truly). They also often have very strict baggage policies – and you have to pay to check any bags at all, often at a sum that's a third or half of the airfare itself. Ryanair, for example, charges up to €40 for the first checked bag up to 15kg (33lbs). (While non-budget airlines, like Alitalia, will allow you a checked bag, the weight allowance will still be smaller than what you can bring on a transatlantic flight; always check before you book your ticket).

If you are booking two back-to-back flights this way, you also need to be aware that if something happens to your first, long-haul flight, like a delay, the airline for your second flight won't be liable (although your travel insurance, or credit card carrying travel insurance, may cover the cost). So give yourself a long lag time in between flights.

You also will need to triple-check which airports you're flying in and out of when you book: Some cities (like London, Paris and even Rome itself) have two or more major airports, often very far from one another.

All that said, if you plan to travel light and you're happy to undergo extra hassles for an extra $100 or $200 in your pocket, it's worth looking into. Just make sure to *always* read the fine print.

2) Don't be afraid to fly into Ciampino

If you're coming directly from abroad, you'll fly into Fiumicino-Leonardo da Vinci (FCO), Rome's international airport. If you're considering my above tip, though, then don't shy away from a European flight just because it flies into Ciampino. In fact, Ciampino can be an even better bet than Fiumicino.

Yes, Ciampino is out of the city center. But so is Fiumicino. And, even though there isn't a train station *right* at the airport at

Ciampino (like there is at Fiumicino), that doesn't mean you have to take a taxi. Instead, several buses take you right into Rome in about 40 minutes, depending on traffic. (See the later section on getting to and from Rome's airports into the center for more details).

3) Don't just look at the websites everyone knows...

...Such as Expedia, Kayak and Priceline. I've found some of my best flight deals on other, European sites, especially vayama.com and mobissimo.com.

4) Get an idea of when the best flights are on a consolidator website, but book directly with the airline itself

Aggregator sites are a great way to get a sense of what you'll have to pay to fly, when – but there may be a surcharge for the privilege. If you see a flight you like, go directly to the airline's website to book it.

5) Don't come in high season

Yes, I covered this before. But it bears mentioning again. If you're looking at flights to Rome and they're all out of your price range, search for the same flight in late October or November. Or February or March. The prices may just be low enough to tempt you out of coming in high season – if my scare tactics about the long lines and heat weren't enough.

If you're all booked for your flight to Rome and you're not planning on taking any trains in Italy, skip the next part and head right to the section on accommodation. Curious about trains? Then read on.

How (and why) to book train tickets

If you're coming to Rome from another city in Italy, 99% of the time, you'll want to take the train. Don't believe the stereotypes about strikes and general unreliability: While strikes can happen and trains can be late, the train system in Italy is far cheaper, better-connected and more reliable than many other parts of the world, but especially the United States.

To get between cities, you can choose between Trenitalia (trenitalia.com), the national rail service, or ItaloTreno (italotreno.it), Italy's newer, high-speed rail service. I'd recommend taking a look at both to compare dates, times and prices.

Although you can buy your ticket when you get to the station, there are benefits to booking online, in advance, from the comfort of your home – particularly if you know what date, and roughly what time, you want to arrive in Rome. The further in advance you book, the better chance you have of finding a promotional, discounted fare. And, of course, the less your risk of not being able to book a seat on a certain train. The downside is that you then have to make that train – if you're late or miss it, you have to change your reservation online or at the desk. Though some tickets allow for reservation changes for free, that can be a hassle, so if you can't be quite sure when you'll make the train, sometimes it's best to wait.

Navigating the ItaloTreno site is fairly straightforward. Trenitalia – which has more speed, class and price options – is a little more complicated, so this is the website that I'll walk you through here.

First, click the button that says "English" at the top right... but know that that won't solve all of your problems. Although much of the site then becomes English, the train station names themselves remain in Italian. So if you type in "Rome", for example, you will find yourself empty-handed. You have to type "Roma" instead.

This can be confusing, so in case you don't know them already, here's a list of Italy's major cities in English, in Italian, and their main train station (which will probably be the one you want to pick, unless you're at accommodation outside of the center):

Rome –> Roma –> Roma Termini
Naples –> Napoli –> Napoli Centrale
Florence –> Firenze –> Firenze S. M. Novella

Venice –> Venezia S. Lucia (on the island) or Venezia Mestre (on the mainland)

Milan –> Milano –> Milano Centrale

Genoa –> Genova –> Genova Piazza Principe

La Spezia –> La Spezia –> La Spezia Centrale

Pisa –> Pisa –> Pisa Centrale

Once you have your destination and date down, you'll often still have a number of options for exactly which train to take. You'll notice clear differences under "length of journey," with some (more expensive) trains being much faster than the other trains. You can also look at "train category". The Frecciarossa, Frecciargento and Frecciabianca trains are fastest, with speeds of up to 120-150mph (200-250km/hr). These are also the most expensive trains and connect only between Italy's major cities. The most economical option tends to be the Intercity trains, which connect everywhere else, make more stops, and are slower, or the Regional (local) trains.

What train you pick, of course, is up to you. But because the high-speed trains tend to be not only faster, but more comfortable and cleaner, when I have a little cash to spare, they're my transport of choice. That's especially true when there are discounts on those trains – as there often are.

Finally, be aware that, if you book your ticket online, you don't need a printer to print it out. Instead, Trenitalia has electronic tickets, either via email or text message on your phone. Once you board, you'll simply show the email or text message to the conductor.

More on what to know about taking the train – and arriving in Rome's train station – later.

What kind of accommodation should you choose?

Take it from someone who's pounded the pavement, researching accommodation for various magazine and newspaper articles and blog posts: Rome has a *ton* of hotels, not to mention

B&Bs, inns, hostels, and apartments. That means the first question to ask yourself is what type of accommodation you'd prefer.

Most people automatically begin researching hotels, and for many travelers, hotels remain the best option. But they're not the best for everyone. Here are four alternatives you may not have considered.

1) Short-term apartment rentals

If you're traveling as a family, don't need a concierge or 24-hour room service (which, by the way, not all hotels in Rome have anyway), and/or want the option of eating in, an apartment rental might be for you.

Luckily, long gone are the days when intrepid travelers had to rely on Craigslist and the honesty of others to arrange such a thing. Now, thanks to sites like airbnb.com, housetrip.com and wimdu.com, a lot of the pain (and anxiety) has been taken out of the process. You can scour photographs, read reviews by other travelers (who, since they booked through the site, definitely did stay there), and (after you've booked) contact the owner by email or phone.

If you do decide to reserve an apartment this way, safeguards are built into the system. With Airbnb, for example, you pay Airbnb itself as soon as you book. But the money isn't released to the owner until after you check in, just in case there are any problems. Airbnb also keeps the security deposit rather than give it to the owner directly.

Other advantages: An apartment rental tends to be way cheaper than comparable hotel rooms. (You can rent an apartment that sleeps four in the city center for about €100; good luck finding two doubles in a hotel that each cost just €50!). If you have picky eaters in the family, want to save money by not eating out constantly, or simply want the option of a cooked breakfast (not always available at hotels or B&Bs), you have a kitchen at your disposal.

Finally, apartment rentals aren't limited to long-term stays. While some apartments have three-night minimums, most places listed accept even one-night stays.

2) **Bed-and-breakfasts, guesthouses, residences, and** *pensioni*

These used to all be called "*pensioni.*" Now, perhaps because of the *pensione's* cheap-and-dowdy stereotype, they're calling themselves by different names.

While some remain cheap (and look it), others are luxurious, pricey, and in Rome's swankiest locations. What they have in common is this: They're usually tiny, with a maximum of five or six rooms. So you'll probably come across the other guests, and you'll probably be greeted by the owner. They also usually have some kind of breakfast option, although whether it's a home-cooked spread or simply a Nespresso machine and some plastic-wrapped croissants is luck of the draw.

Overall, these tend to be a little more economical than a comparable room at a boutique hotel – and more intimate.

In general, some of the most atmospheric and delightful "hotels" I've seen have been in this category.

3) **Hostels**

There are a handful of hostels in Rome, most of them in the fairly-safe-but-pretty-dingy Termini area. They're much like hostels you'd see worldwide, favored by the young and by backpackers. One exception is The Beehive, a mixed hostel/hotel with an eco-conscious attitude, super-friendly owners, and cute, colorful rooms.

4) **Convents and monasteries**

Rome has dozens of convents or monasteries, and many take guests. This is a creative option for the budget-conscious – or merely curious.

On the plus side, they're often very economical, the buildings can be historic and atmospheric, and they couldn't be more tranquil. On the other hand, remember that most have curfews (often at 10 or 11pm, early for a city where most people eat dinner at 9pm). Most take guests of any religious persuasion, but you will be staying in a strongly Catholic environment. Receptionists' (and nuns', or monks') English might be negligible. And the rooms can be rather spartan.

Whatever type of accommodation you book, do just do yourself one favor. Don't stay in the kind of hotel that you could easily stay in in Boston, or Toronto, or London. There are hundreds of independently-run hotels in Rome, many of which are just as fantastic – and which have just as many amenities – as a Hilton or Marriott. Besides, what's the charm in walking into your hotel room in Rome… and feeling like you could be *anywhere else* in the world?

Finally, don't worry that if you don't book an American chain hotel, you'll be forced to speak in Italian. Anyone manning a hotel desk in Rome will have enough English to answer your questions.

Which neighborhood should you stay in?

Once you've decided what type of accommodation you're going to consider, it's time to think about your neighborhood.

In general, most tourists want to stay in the *centro storico*. With reason. The historic center is home to most of Rome's major sights, and it's where that picture-perfect version of Rome – the Rome of cobblestoned streets, colorful *palazzi* and lovely piazzas – exists. It's where most of the main sights are. And it's not only easily walkable, but well-connected by bus and (to a lesser extent) metro.

If all that sounds great, then first, don't get tripped up on what *is* the *centro storico*. Technically, it's the area of Rome surrounded by the city's 3rd-century Aurelian walls. If you're looking at a map of Rome, start at the Vatican. Going clockwise, the walls encircle the Vatican up to the Lepanto metro stop, across the river to Piazza del Popolo, and east as far as the Castro Pretorio metro stop. They continue south to encompass Termini station and the Basilica of San Giovanni in Laterano, the Baths of Caracalla, and Circus Maximus (running just north of the Piramide metro stop), where they head across the river due west of the Circo Massimo metro stop and take in a sliver of Trastevere.

However, not all parts of the *centro storico* are made equal. Each neighborhood has a different atmosphere. And if walking out your door and into a living postcard is your goal, then you'll want to be particularly choosy.

Here's a quick rundown of what to expect in each area. I've also added some of my favorite hotels in each quarter. $ means under €125 (for two, in low season); $$ is between €125-€200; and $$$ is €201 and up.

The heart of the *centro storico*

This isn't technically a neighborhood, but I'm using it as shorthand for the central area that most people think of when they think "Rome" – the triangle with Piazza del Popolo at its northern point, the Spanish Steps and Trevi Fountain to the east, and the Pantheon and Piazza Navona to the west. Beautiful, atmospheric and convenient to the sights, this area is where most people want to stay.

Of course, it's also where hotels are the most expensive, where the streets crowd with tourists and shoppers, and where 99% of restaurants are overpriced and mediocre. On the other hand, every corner looks like a postcard. You win some, you lose some.

Favorite hotels: Best Pantheon B&B ($), Relais Maddalena ($$), Locanda del Sole ($$), Suite Sistina ($$), Babuino 181 ($$$), Mario de Fiori 37 ($$$), Margutta 57 ($$$), Gigli d'Oro Suites ($$$), Spagna Royal Suite ($$$), Crossing Condotti ($$$), Hotel Raphael ($$$)

Via Veneto, Barberini and Repubblica

The winding Via Veneto is famous for its hotels, some of which are five-star. But most seem, at least to me, to be huge and overpriced. Meanwhile, the rest of the northeastern corner of the historic center, especially near the Barberini and Repubblica metro stops, feels like a big city. For the most part, forget cobblestones and quaint churches; this is where the buildings are tall, the streets wide, and the passersby businesslike.

Favorite hotels: Leon's Place ($$$), Baglioni Hotel Regina ($
$$)

Termini and the Esquiline

Although some hoteliers diplomatically call this neighborhood
Monti (a lovely, trendy *rione* I'll get to in a minute), anything from
Piazza Vittorio Emanuele to Santa Maria Maggiore and northeast
to the Termini train station is, more properly, the Esquiline hill.
The neighborhood here tends to feel gritty and look grungy
(although there are some lovely corners, too!). In general, this is
where you'll see immigrants hawking counterfeited purses,
homeless people huddling in corners, and garbage littering the
street. It's also where you'll find many of Rome's cheapest hotels,
hostels and B&Bs.

The area tends to be perfectly safe – Rome is, as a whole, *much*
safer when it comes to muggings and violent crimes than pretty
much any city in America, as well as Dublin, London and Paris
(more on that later) – but it may not be what you imagined when
you first pictured Rome.

Favorite hotels: The Beehive ($), Aldebaran Bed and
Breakfast ($)

Monti

In ancient times, this *rione* was the red-light district, home to
gladiators and prostitutes (Julius Caesar even moved there to show
he was "one of the people"). Today, it's a gorgeous little
neighborhood filled with medieval *palazzi*, cobblestoned streets, and
an eclectic mix of traditional *trattorie* and hip boutiques. The small
size means there aren't many hotels here, so don't forget to
consider options like apartments, too.

If you want to stay here, look at the area bordered by Via
Nazionale (to the west), Santa Maria Maggiore (to the north), the
Colle Oppio park (to the east), and the Roman forum and
Colosseum (to the south).

Favorite hotels: Hotel de Monti ($), Nicolas Inn ($), The Inn at the Roman Forum ($$), Residenza Torre Colonna ($$)

Celio

Further southwest of Monti is Celio, another *rione* with a strong history. The couple of blocks right around the Colosseum tend to be touristy and busy during the day, but the rest of this area, which stretches southeast to the Basilica of San Giovanni in Laterano, feels quiet and residential.

Favorite hotels: Aklesia Suites ($), RetRome Colosseum B&B ($), Hotel Capo d'Africa ($$), Hotel Palazzo Manfredi ($$$)

Aventine

This hill, just south of the Circus Maximus, is home to some of the loveliest streets and homes in Rome. Its small size and exclusivity mean there are few hotels and B&Bs here. It also doesn't feel like it's "in the middle" of anything, thanks to its greenery and the fact that it's at least a 15-minute walk to most of the major sights. Since hotels are scarce, this is a place to look for alternative types of accommodation.

Favorite hotels: Hotel Sant'Anselmo ($$)

Forum Boarium

This itty-bitty neighborhood is tucked just to the south and west of Circus Maximus. It has some wonderful sights – including the Church of San Giorgio in Velabro, the Arch of Janus, and the Church of San Nicola in Carcere – and it's just a three-minute walk to the Jewish Ghetto and Piazza Venezia. It's also tranquil, lovely and off the beaten path.

Favorite hotels: Fortyseven Hotel ($$), Kolbe Hotel ($$$)

Campo dei Fiori and the Jewish Ghetto

From Piazza Venezia to the Tiber, you've got beautiful ancient ruins, the Jewish Ghetto, lively Campo dei Fiori, and my favorite piazza in Rome, Piazza Farnese. This district has the atmosphere (and history) of the area around Piazza Navona and the Pantheon, with far fewer crowds.

Favorite hotels: Maison Giulia ($), Hotel Campo de Fiori ($
$), DOM Hotel ($$$)

Trastevere

Just over the Tiber from Campo dei Fiori and the Ghetto is
Trastevere, an atmospheric district that, today, is as likely to be
home to American study-abroad students, expats and wealthy
Italians as the working-class and bohemian Romans it once
housed. Still, the neighborhood remains charming, with lots of
corners and tiny streets where life is still lived much as it would
have been decades ago. *Favorite hotels:* WRH Trastevere ($),
Residenza Santa Maria ($), Il Boom B&B ($), Guesthouse Arco dei
Tolomei ($$), Worldhotel Ripa Roma ($$), Donna Camilla Savelli
Hotel ($$$)

Prati

If you find the center of Rome's *centro storico* too confusing and
chaotic, consider Prati. This area around the Vatican, just over the
river from sights like Piazza Navona and Piazza del Popolo, was
laid out in the 19th century, so its grid system and wide boulevards
look more continental and, well, organized than the rest of Rome.

While the area right around the Vatican museums and St.
Peter's is extremely touristy, once you get a little farther away,
authentic restaurants and the rhythm of daily life in Rome abound.
It also becomes easier to find cheaper accommodation.

Favorite hotels: Rome Armony Suites ($), B&B A Peace of
Rome ($), Hotel Farnese ($$), ISA Design Hotel ($$)

Testaccio

Just south of the Aventine, the Testaccio quarter is one of the
least touristy in Rome – and has some of the best restaurants and
bakeries in the city. The ancient area, which gets its name from
Monte Testaccio, a hill that came about first as a dump for ancient
Roman amphorae, can feel more modern and gritty than the
center of the city. But it's perfectly safe, cheaper than the center,
and convenient: Thanks to the metro and many buses, you're just 5

or 10 minutes away from Trastevere, the Colosseum, and the heart of the historic center.

There are few hotels, so this is another area to look at alternative accommodation options like Airbnb.

Favorite hotels: Althea Inn ($)

Outside of the historic center: Parioli

If you're looking for a neighborhood that feels civilized, European, *and* off the beaten tourist path, consider Parioli. This upmarket, residential area, just north of the Villa Borghese and the *centro storico*, is starting to come alive with new restaurants and shops. And thanks to its location near both the Villa Borghese and Villa Ada, two of Rome's biggest parks, it's ideal if you're a jogger or just looking for some green space.

The downside is that there isn't a convenient metro stop, so you'll have to rely on buses, which are frequent and connect Parioli to the heart of the center, or on taxis.

Favorite hotels: Villa Paganini B&B ($), Lord Byron Hotel ($$$)

Sights to book in advance

It doesn't matter how much you're willing to go with the flow, or how much more interested you are in people-watching and shopping than sightseeing: When it comes to sightseeing in Rome, it pays to think ahead.

After all, if it's your first time to Rome, you probably want to visit the Colosseum, the Vatican museums, and St. Peter's Basilica. And you probably don't want to stand in line for two hours to get inside. And when you're inside… you probably want to have a good experience.

Plus, if it's your second, third, or tenth time in Rome (or even if it's your first), you probably want to see some of the most exciting "new" sites (or rather, newly-opened ancient sites) that the city has to offer.

Both of those options require a little bit of planning.

First, some of Rome's most rewarding sights – including the Borghese Gallery, Palazzo Valentini, St. Peter's tomb, the underground of the Colosseum and the Domus Aurea – aren't things you can simply show up to. You *must* book in advance.

Second, major sights like the Colosseum and Vatican have *long* lines in high season. You will need a plan if you want to avoid waiting. Although you might be able to get away with winging it in low season – which remember, for Rome, is only from November through February (excluding Christmas) – that's not a guarantee. Depending on the time of day, there can still be lines.

Don't worry that we don't go into why these sights are special below. We'll talk about that later.

Also later, I will give you some options for how to skip the line at the Colosseum, Vatican museums and Sistine Chapel, and St. Peter's Basilica if you (oops!) forgot to book in advance. But while they'll shorten your time waiting, they may not get rid of it altogether. For that, here are the only surefire options for…:

The Colosseum

Who doesn't want to visit the Colosseum when they're in Rome? Maybe you, when you walk up for the first time and see the 3-hour line to buy tickets. Here are three ways to avoid it. (Do keep in mind that here, as at the Vatican museums and St. Peter's Basilica, security screenings – a recent addition for the Colosseum – as well as a limit to the number of people allowed in means that, even for ticket-holders, there may be delays… but it's still nothing like what you'd see if you have to buy tickets).

Reserve your ticket online in advance

You can purchase your combined ticket to the Colosseum, Forum, and Palatine Hill in advance at coopculture.com. You get one entrance to each site, and can use it over two days. Assuming you don't have a Roma Pass, OmniaPass or a tour booked, there's really no reason not to do this, particularly as it doesn't pin you down to a specific date (you just have to use it by the end of the calendar year).

Coopculture, the site I have linked to above, is the official website for Rome's archaeological sites; you should never buy a ticket online using any other site, since at best all they'll do is add a surcharge for the privilege. The combined Colosseum/Forum/Palatine ticket, which is the only option, costs €12 at the door, and booking it online costs just €2 extra. You can either print out your ticket at home or pick it up at the site; print it out to avoid any potential wait to pick up tickets.

Book a tour in advance

Any independent tour company worth their salt (and *always* cross-check with reviews on Tripadvisor) will include skip-the-line access to the Colosseum. (Find out more about how to decide whether to book a tour, and which types to check out, later).

Buy a Roma Pass or OmniaPass

There are plenty of situations in which these cards, which start at a hefty €28 per person, don't pay off. (Later, I'll help you decide if a Roma Pass or OmniaPass might be right for you). But if you opt to buy one, then you'll get to benefit from one of its major bonuses: It lets you skip any ticket-buying lines including the one at the Colosseum, no advance reservations needed.

The Colosseum underground

The Colosseum underground opened to much excitement back in 2010 – including with blog posts and an article in the *Guardian* by yours truly. It was the first time the underground was opened to the public, and because it shows you the tunnels and rooms where animals and gladiators would have waited for their turns to fight, it is a pretty cool, and different, thing to see – particularly if you've been to the Colosseum before. The experience also includes a visit out onto the arena floor and up to the third tier, which, like the underground, otherwise are closed to the general public.

Why am I listing this separately from the Colosseum? Because the process of getting in is different. As it is a particularly delicate archaeological area, the number of visitors is limited, and unlike the rest of the Colosseum, you can only see these parts on a guided tour.

Before you get too excited, check coopculture.com to make sure the underground will be open during your visit: It can close in winter and at other times, including on short notice, thanks to inclement weather.

Assuming it is open, there are three main options for accessing the underground. These are:

Colosseum underground tour, with a Colosseum guide

This is the cheapest option. It's also the riskiest. The first potential issue is the guide; although the "official" Colosseum guides tend to know their stuff, they also give the same tour over and over, for months on end — so their enthusiasm often seems to have worn a bit thin. Many also don't have stellar English.

The second issue is that, likely thanks to the underground's popularity, it's becoming increasingly byzantine to book directly with Coopculture. The good news is you can do it yourself, online. The bad news is you can only book on the third Monday of the month, for the following month. (In other words, Monday, 15 May for the month of June 2017). But as with any kinds of details like these, which in Italy can frequently change or be contradictory (for example, one of the open dates isn't actually a Monday, but a Tuesday...), do double-check on the Coopculture booking page.

The tours, which are given in English, Italian and Spanish, cost €9. In addition to buying the tour in advance, *you now must also book your own Colosseum entrance ticket* (the tour does not include it). So make sure you do that in advance, as well (see section above).

Colosseum, Forum and Palatine tour, with an independent guide

This is the tour offered by Walks of Italy (walksofitaly.com). (Other companies do the same tour, but hand their groups over to an official Colosseum guide for the underground part). In this version, you get a complete tour of the Colosseum, Forum and Palatine with the same fluent English-speaking, animated guide. Cost: €74.

Colosseum, Forum and Palatine tour, with a Colosseum guide for the underground part

This tour is offered by Dark Rome (darkrome.com), among others. You get a complete tour of the ancient city with a fluent English-speaking guide; however, you're handed over to one of those official Colosseum guides for the underground. Therefore, the tour group has a maximum size of 10 people, but 25 in the underground. Cost: €92.

The Domus Aurea

In 2014, the Golden House of Nero reopened to the public. Whether you're an ancient Rome lover or an archaeology nerd, this was (and remains) a huge deal. As with the Colosseum underground, the Domus Aurea is a delicate site and isn't guaranteed to be open. Always check in advance, which you can do at coopculture.com.

Domus Aurea tour

You can only visit the site on a guided tour; led by archaeologists, these take place (in English, Italian, French and Spanish) on Saturdays and Sundays only. In an exciting new development, as of this year, the tours have a twist: Virtual reality headsets that recreate what it all would have looked like. The cost is €16 (including a €2 reservation fee). Book online in advance at coopculture.com.

The Vatican museums and Sistine Chapel

The Vatican museums (which also are home to the Sistine Chapel) are a must-see. And since everyone seems to agree on that point, there are long lines here, too. But again, there's no reason to stand in one. (Although, as for the Colosseum, you may need to queue up for the required security check). Instead, you can:

Reserve your ticket online in advance

The cheapest option (it's an extra €4 on top of the ticket price, which is €16 for an adult), this is also very easy. You can book directly on the Vatican museums website (muscivaticani.va). Although it says "Tour Itineraries", don't worry: You don't have to book a guided tour, it's just an imperfect translation. (If you want a ticket only, you'll select the "Open Tour" option on the following page). You'll also notice a plethora of other fancy options – including night visits and tours of the Vatican Gardens – which are worth checking out, but if all you want are the main highlights (i.e. the Raphael Rooms, Sistine Chapel and museums), select "Open tour of the Vatican museums and Sistine Chapel".

Particularly in high season, try to do this at least a couple of weeks in advance. You can then bring either a printout of the ticket, or show it on your smartphone or tablet, to the guards at the entrance. You're also supposed to bring an I.D., though it's rarely checked (it will be, though, if you've bought a reduced-price ticket, such as one for students). While you'll have a specific entry time, the guards tend to be lax if you show up a little late, so don't worry too much if you're running a bit behind.

Buy an OmniaPass

To be honest, I doubt this pass is ever worth it. (More on that later). But I'm mentioning it because, unlike the Roma Pass, it does include entry to the Vatican museums. If that's your major reason for getting it, though, you should just buy a Vatican ticket in advance, as per the above. Find out more about the OmniaPass on their website (romeandvaticanpass.com).

Book a tour in advance with the Vatican

You can book a tour with an official Vatican guide directly through the museum website (muscivaticani.va). This is the cheapest tour option – but, as with the Colosseum, many of these guides have given the same tour for years, meaning their enthusiasm level can be a little bit low.

Book a tour in advance with an independent operator

Same deal as the Colosseum: Any independent tour company worth their salt will include skip-the-line access to the Vatican museums. (More about tours later).

St. Peter's Basilica

St. Peter's Basilica is free to enter, and you don't need a ticket. You do, though, need to go through a security check. In high season, the line for that alone often stretches around the piazza... and there's no shade, so in summer, that can be both a frustrating and sweaty prospect.

But just because there's no ticket required doesn't mean that you can't reserve a ticket in advance to help you get around the security line. Confusing, I know, but here's why: There is an alternate exit from the Sistine Chapel that leads directly onto the porch of St. Peter's Basilica. Because anyone in the Sistine Chapel already has gone through the Vatican museums security check, there's no second check there. Although you can sneakily try to use that exit (more later), there's only one surefire way to do so, and that is...

Book a tour of the Vatican museums

Always read the fine print, but most official and independent Vatican tours end at the porch of St. Peter's Basilica. Result: You've already skipped the basilica line.

St. Peter's tomb

Thanks to its ancient mosaic and fresco, the necropolis under St. Peter's Basilica – which includes what's thought to be the tomb of St. Peter – makes a super-cool visit for anyone, not just pilgrims. But because the archaeological site is delicate, only 250 visitors can enter per day, on tours only, and must book in advance. Note that visitors also must be at least 15 years old.

Vatican scavi tour

Unlike the other sights here, the Vatican necropolis, also called the "scavi" (Italian for "excavations"), hasn't exactly joined the 21st century in terms of booking options. To reserve tickets, you have to email scavi@fsp.va or fax +39 0669873017. You also can ask at the Excavations Office when you're in Rome, but because these tours tend to book out weeks in advance, it's advised that you don't wait until then to do so. Make sure to include the number of participants, names, which language you need, how to contact you, and the period when you're available to attend.

Tickets cost €13, and unlike the other sights in this section, there are no reduced-price tickets for students, children, teachers, tour guides or anyone else.

Borghese Gallery

This is my favorite art museum in Rome, and it's absolutely a must-see. Filled with some of the finest, and most moving, sculptures and paintings in the world – including by Raphael, Rubens, Titian, Canova, Caravaggio and Bernini – skipping the Borghese is like visiting Paris and dismissing the Musée d'Orsay. To keep it a pleasant experience, however (and to protect the art), the museum limits the number of people who can be inside at any one time. Entrances are at 9am, 11am, 1pm, 3pm, and 5pm, daily except Monday. Because of the museum's popularity, entrances can sell out quickly; book at least two or three weeks in advance.

Here are your (only) options for access:

Reserve your ticket online in advance

Book directly through the Borghese Gallery on their website (galleriaborghese.it). Tickets cost €15 for adults, which includes a €2 reservation fee. (If you have a Roma Pass or OmniaPass and are visiting the Borghese Gallery as one of your free sites, you don't need to buy this ticket, but you do still need to book. You can't do it online, but instead must call +39 0632810).

Book a tour of the Borghese Gallery

Starting to sound familiar? You also can automatically get a reservation by booking a tour with a reputable tour company or by taking an official tour with the Borghese Gallery itself.

Palazzo Farnese

This palace, which happens to be on my favorite piazza in Rome (of the same name), is a little-known gem. With head architects including both Michelangelo and Giacomo della Porta, this was the opulent Renaissance residence of the later Pope Paul III. Its interior decorations are only visible on a guided tour, and for art lovers, they're well worth seeing: In Rome, the 16th-century ceiling frescoes by Annibale Carracci are rivaled only by the Sistine Chapel.

After years of only Italian and French tours, in 2012, the embassy began giving weekly tours of the palace in English.

Palazzo Farnese tour

English tours are currently offered every Wednesday at 5pm; tours are also held in Italian and French. Registration closes a week in advance, and children under 10 are not admitted. The cost is €5. You must book online in advance (inventerrome.com).

Palazzo Valentini

If the Borghese is my favorite art museum, this is my favorite ancient, underground site.

Palazzo Valentini tour

Tours are given several times a day in English, Italian, French, German and Spanish. You must book in advance, which you can do online (palazzovalentini.it). The visit, which takes about an hour and a half, costs €13.50 for adults. Particularly in high season or if you have limited time, I'd recommend booking this at least a month in advance – this is now one of Rome's most popular sights.

Imperial Forum light shows

In 2015, Rome launched a nighttime light show in the Imperial Forum (Fori Imperiali) at the Forum of Augustus. It was so successful that the following year, the city not only brought the show back – it also began a second one, at the Forum of Caesar.

Both experiences lead visitors through a usually-inaccessible archaeological site: The Imperial Forum, which was built by Caesar and the emperors who followed him and which, unlike the Republican Forum on the other side of the Via dei Fori Imperiali, you can't buy a ticket to wander through. The shows not only give you access, but bring the ruins to life: The automated (and well-done) voiceover, through headphones, provides the stories behind what you're seeing, while lights illuminate the ruins around you, re-drawing various sections as you go – allowing you to see the Forum as if you were an ancient Roman, doing your shopping with friends or heading to a temple to pray.

The shows run outside of winter only, and dates are being released on a year by year basis. For 2017, both shows run from 13 April to 12 November. They depart every 20 minutes, are offered in eight languages (including English). Although you can buy tickets in person when you arrive, I would recommend booking online in advance to ensure your spot, particularly in high season; there is a €1 surcharge per tour for pre-booking. You can buy your tickets online (viaggioneifori.it).

Roma Pass, OmniaPass, Archaeologia Card... oh my

Once upon a time, Rome had one combined sightseeing pass, called the Roma Pass, for tourists who wanted to skip lines and use public transport. Those were simpler days.

Now, there's a somewhat dizzying array of options. Not only does the Roma Pass now have a 48-hour and a 72-hour version, but it has competitors: The Rome City Pass, confusingly also called the TurboPass, which includes the Vatican (but you'll pay a premium for the addition); the Omnia Vatican & Rome card, which also includes the Vatican (but will charge you even more); and the Archaeologia Card (refreshingly bells-and-whistles free and which focuses on Rome's ancient archaeological sites). Though what they offer varies, all of them promise skip-the-line benefits to some of Rome's most popular sites.

If you already feel overwhelmed by the choice, I can make it simple for you: Despite the fact that some are better deals than others, you probably aren't going to want any of them. The reason: They're all pricier versions of what you can already achieve on your own – often fairly easily. You can take care of the line-skipping aspect by booking sights in advance (and, in a pinch, using the tricks we'll talk about later). And not only do most people find they tend to use public transport less frequently than they'd expect, but if they do want unlimited access for the convenience, they can buy a far more economical version directly from Rome's transport agency. (More in the later section on public transport, but as an example, you can get 72 hours of unlimited transport for €18, while the 72-hour Roma Pass costs €38.50).

Finally, the cards often overhype what they include. One example: The Omnia says it includes free entrance to the Colosseum and to the Forum/Palatine. But the two sites are *already* on the same single, combined ticket, which as you know from before, you can book yourself for €14. Worse, they can be downright price-gouging. Most charge you (sometimes the same as an adult price) for a child's card. And yet under-18's already get into free at state-run sites (including the Colosseum), and under-10's go for free on public transport when accompanied by adults.

Still curious? Here's more about each type of pass, and the (relatively rare) circumstances in which you might want each type.

Roma Pass

The classic option, this now has two versions. The **48-hour**

Roma Pass gets you free entrance to the first museum or archaeological site that you visit (except for the Vatican museums and Sistine Chapel, which aren't part of the Roma Pass network), unlimited public transport for two days, and (relatively minor) discounts at sites across Rome. It costs €28.50.

The only difference with the **72-hour Roma Pass** is that you have free entrance to the first two sights you visit, not one, plus three days of public transport. It costs €38.50.

Neither of the passes gives discounts for children. And, as noted above, keep in mind that adults can buy their own 24-hour public transport pass for €7, 48-hour pass for €12.50 and 72-hour for €18 (plus that children under 10 ride for free). Aside from that, whether this is worth it for you depends on which sights you want to visit – and how much you value convenience. But as a general rule of thumb…

The Roma Pass may not be worth it for you if:
•You're in one of the categories of visitors who already receive free entrance to the sights. Though it's smart to double-check each site individually, for state-run museums and archaeological areas, like the Colosseum, this includes children under 18 years old, along with university students or teachers (even non-European) who are studying subjects like archaeology or art history who have a valid certificate of enrollment or document for the current academic year.

•You're in a category who receives discounted entrance to sights. Again, double-check – but this often applies to, for example, European students between 18 and 25 years old.

•You're already planning to take tours which include the entrances to sights.

•You're not planning to visit a more expensive sight (for the 48-hour pass) or two of the more expensive sights (for the 72-hour pass).

•You're traveling on a budget. Even if you plan to use a great deal of public transport and visit two of the priciest sites, you'll likely still spend a few more euros on the Roma Pass.

The Roma Pass may be worth it for you if:

•You're not doing guided tours, you'll be paying full-price entrances to sights and you're organized enough to visit your two most expensive sights first.

•You're a fan of spending a little bit more money to save time. Instead of, say, buying a 72-hour public transport pass, plus booking the Colosseum online in advance, plus buying your ticket at the Capitoline Museums, you can buy one Roma Pass and get all three done at once.

You can buy the Roma Pass online or when you arrive in Rome; sale points include the Termini and Spagna metro stations and any participating museum or sight. Check romapass.it for the full list.

Rome City Pass (aka Turbopass)

The Rome City Pass offers more sights than the Roma Pass, but less value. It includes unlimited public transport for the time you buy. It also includes free entrance to the Vatican Museums and Sistine Chapel (a maximum €20 value), the Colosseum/Forum/Palatine (€14 value), and to a handful of other less popular sights, like the Baths of Caracalla. You'll save on some others.

It also includes audioguides for the Vatican museums and St. Peter's Basilica (neither of which are much to write home about), and a hop-on, hop-off sightseeing bus tour with one of two operators (but for only 1.5 to 2 hours, which seems sort of pointless, particularly as it's the rare time indeed I've ever heard rave reviews about the information given on a bus tour). (More about bus tours later).

For an adult, that will cost you €89.90 for the two-day pass, €99.90 for the three-day (which also includes free entrance to Castel Sant'Angelo) or €159.90 for the six-day version (which also includes free entrance to Castel Sant'Angelo, the Borghese Gallery plus to sites along the Appia Antica).

Interestingly, the Turbopass is the only of these full-package passes that's relatively honest about how much children cost. A child's card costs €28.50 for two days, €29.90 for three days and €29.90 for six days – making it more reasonable for kids, actually, than the Roma Pass.

Particularly where the adults are concerned, though, work out the math, and you'll find that – even if you were planning to do everything included in the pass – the convenience comes at a cost of another €15 at least. And even if you're a fan of convenience, you could buy the two-day Roma Pass for €28.50, plan to see the Colosseum first to make it free, buy Vatican tickets online for €20 and still have an extra €50 in your pocket to spend on audioguides and, if you really want, a bus tour. I know what I'd go with.

The Turbopass may not be worth it for you if:
•You're most people.

The Turbopass may be worth it for you if:
•You already were planning to do everything offered on the card, including bus tour and audio guides, and you don't mind spending an extra €15-plus for the convenience factor.

You can book the Turbopass online at turbopass.com.

Omnia Vatican & Rome Card

The Omnia Vatican & Rome Card is an even more expensive version of the Rome City Pass – and basically, all you're paying for is a tricked-out package that includes the 72-hour Roma Pass (which on its own, remember, costs €38.50), plus several items aimed at those interested in the Vatican. The only main additions to the Roma Pass are that it includes free entry to the Vatican Museums (on top of the Roma Pass entry to two other sites); the (pretty mediocre) audioguide for St. Peter's Basilica; and that it gives you a hop-on-hop-off bus tour ticket with Roma Cristiana (which is run by the Opera Romana Pellegrinaggi, a group focusing on services for pilgrims) that's good for three days (technically, a €32 value). (More about these bus tours in the next section; you might also want to check out the most recent Tripadvisor reviews of the Roma Cristiana bus before you pull the trigger). It also claims to give you "fast-pass" entrance to St. Peter's Basilica, but this is a bit of sleight of hand: What you actually get is an group audio tour, and while that group does use a side entrance to skip the main line to the basilica (though you still have to go through security), you have to be there at precisely the right time to avoid waiting – because those tours only enter at certain times.

If you were on the fence about the Roma Pass or Turbopass being worth it, though, then this one almost definitely isn't. The Omnia package is the priciest of them all. Currently it costs €113 for an adult, €80 for a child… and children apparently count as only nine years old and under. So yes, your 10-year-old will cost an exorbitant €113, even though they'd get into sites and travel on public transport for free.

Even for adults, if you do the math, it's extremely unlikely that this is worth it. For an adult, including booking fees, the Vatican costs €20, the Colosseum (and Forum and Palatine) are €14, and the Borghese Gallery is €17. A three-day transit pass is €18 and a hop-on hop-off bus is €30. That's €99 total, saving you €14, and that's assuming you're going to do all of the main things on the list – including both public transit and a hop-on hop-off bus, simultaneously.

The Omnia card may not be worth it for you if:
•You're most people.

The Omnia card may be worth it for you if:
•You plan to do everything offered on the card – including the bus tour – and you don't mind spending an extra €15-plus for the convenience factor.

You can buy the Omnia pass at romeandvaticanpass.com.

Archaeologia Card

This card is exactly what it says it is, it isn't fancy, it's the cheapest of the lot – but unless you're planning to visit some of Rome's off-the-beaten-path archaeological sites, it's still unlikely to be worth it.

Good for seven days, it includes access to many of Rome's main archaeological sites and museums, including the Colosseum/ Palatine/Forum (a maximum €14 value); the Palazzo Massimo, Crypta Balbi, Palazzo Altemps and the Baths of Diocletian (which are all on one combined €7 ticket anyway); and the Baths of Caracalla along with some of the sites along the Appia Antica (which are on a combined €6 ticket). The ticket costs €23 adults, €13 reduced.

The Archaeologia card may not be worth it for you if:

•You're planning on visiting the Colosseum, but not lesser-known sites like the Palazzo Massimo or Baths of Caracalla (although you should!).

The Archaeologia card may be worth it for you if:

•If you're going to one site from each of the three categories above – for example, the Colosseum plus Palazzo Massimo plus Baths of Caracalla – you'll save €4 per adult.

You can buy the Archaeologia card at any of the sites themselves, so you can make a game-day decision of whether to go for it or not.

To tour or not to tour?

You might have noticed that, for all of these sights save Palazzo Valentini, one good way to skip the line is to book a tour in advance.

Tours might not be the way you usually travel. They're not how I usually travel, either. But in Rome, they're worth considering.

Not so much because Rome is confusing and it's nice to have

someone do the navigation for you. (Although that can be true, and it does help). But, instead, because Rome's history is *so* dense, and so complex, and so *incredible,* that it's very easy to only skim the surface when you're on your own: To walk by 2,000-year-old ruins you don't even notice, or to pass over a church that you only realize later, reading your guidebook back in your hotel room, hid a Michelangelo statue or 9th-century mosaics.

Plus, Rome's stories are what make the city come alive. The Forum, for example, practically hums with tales of sex and intrigue, treachery and blood. Oh, you can't hear that "hum" by simply walking around these ruins, squinting at a map, trying to figure out which temple is which? That's where a (good) tour guide comes in.

Something else to keep in mind is that most of Rome's archaeological sites and its museums are *not* that great with signage. In the Vatican museums and Borghese Gallery, for example, you'll get a little placard next to the painting with the title, artist, and year... maybe. But that's it.

Finally, when I say you might want to consider a tour, I'm not thinking of – and definitely not recommending – multi-day package tours. Or bus tours. Or tours that involve big groups of people wearing headsets and a guide waving a big flag. Instead, I'm talking about walking tours, particularly those that are smaller groups.

Of course, you probably don't want to spend your whole time in Rome glued to a tour guide's hip. Nor can most of our budgets support that. Here's help for how to narrow it down.

Hold on. Why a walking tour?

There are a few reasons I recommend smaller-group walking tours, if you're able, over bus tours or driver-guides.

For one, Rome, as mentioned before, is a very walkable city. It's also a city where, to some extent, you *have* to walk in order to see everything it has to offer. Not every street in the city center is open to vehicles, and not all of the streets that are open to traffic will allow buses (thankfully). Even on a hop-on, hop-off bus tour, you'll find that you have to do some walking from your drop-off point to the major actual sites.

For another, few people want to feel herded like cattle when they're in some of the world's most extraordinary sites. But when you're talking about a big tour of 40 people or more, that's exactly what you'll find. Because many of the sites are, themselves, not necessarily that big, that kind of group can be pretty unwieldy.

Overall, I find that walking tours with independent companies tend to be more intimate, interesting and informative than the others. But one of my first jobs in Rome was working with a small-group tour company – so feel free to take that with a grain of salt.

Of course, my one caveat to all of this is if someone in your group isn't particularly mobile and requires an alternative to walking. Because of the convenience of the bus going around and around in a loop, and because it's geared towards tourists and therefore really easy to figure out where you are, doing something like a hop-on hop-off bus can take some of the effort and stress out of getting around.

What should I get a tour of?

Here are some experiences that I would *most* recommend considering with a guide:

An overview of, and introduction to, Rome

Many tour companies have introductory tours to Rome that cover sights like the Trevi Fountain, Pantheon, and Spanish Steps. Since you'll probably see these sights again and again as you walk around Rome, it can be helpful to hear the stories behind them when you first arrive in the city. It's a great way to get other tips about visiting Rome, too.

An aspect of Rome you'll encounter over and over – like food

A food tour can be a great, hands-on way to experience a truly "local" side of Rome. Plus, contrary to popular belief, there's a trick to knowing where to eat and what to order in Rome. By doing a food tour early on, you can start off your trip with real appreciation for Rome's food... plus learn crucial tips for how to pick restaurants and *gelaterie*, how to know which foods are in season, and so on. (Of course, reading the section on eating in Rome helps with all of those, too).

Forum, Palatine, and Colosseum

Unless you're a classics specialist or an archaeologist, it can be hard to figure out what's what in the Forum and Palatine, never mind get a sense of the grandeur and excitement that *should* animate the ruins here. On the other hand, a good guide can really bring the ruins to life. Believe it or not, I think this is especially worth doing with children (as long, again, as you have an entertaining tour guide).

The Vatican museums and Sistine Chapel

The Vatican is overwhelming. Even though it's hard to get lost if you're following the direct route, it is easy to feel lost in the shuffle. And I can't tell you how much more rewarding it is when you step into the Sistine Chapel knowing the drama and importance behind it.

The Borghese Gallery

Not everyone thinks about going to the Borghese, and even fewer people think about getting a tour guide for the gallery. But unless you're an art historian, it can be seriously worthwhile. Admiring pretty paintings and sculptures is one thing; hearing the fascinating stories behind them (how Raphael's Entombment tells the true tale of parricide and a mother's grief! how Caravaggio's paintings might have been so dark because he had just murdered someone!) is another.

That sounds tempting. So, how should I pick a tour company?

When it comes to choosing a tour company, you have an overwhelming number of options.

I used to work for a company called Walks of Italy (walksofitaly.com) which focuses on small-group walking tours (usually under 15 people) and experiences with a twist (like getting into the Sistine Chapel before it opens to the public, or a food tour with a pizza-making class). I still recommend them, and consulting clients I've had who have taken their tours over the years have all come back happy. Another one that gets rave reviews is Context Tours (contexttravel.com), which has very small (maximum six people) group tours and uses only academics as tour guides; as you'd expect, its reputation is for in-depth, cerebral tours that are perfect for the history lovers or amateur archaeologists among us. For food tours, Eating Italy Food Tours (eatingitalyfoodtours.com) was the first dedicated food tour company in Rome and continues to get rave reviews from clients.

But there are a lot of great tour companies in Rome – each offering something a little different. And depending on your budget, your interests and the style you want (laid-back or academic? Kid-friendly or more for adults? In-depth or a little more wham-bam?), you may prefer a different tour company to someone else.

When picking a tour company or private guide, here are some things to think about while you're doing research and reading reviews online (which you should always do, of course, on a site like Tripadvisor, not on the company's own site):

1) Is this actually a tour company?

It sounds like a silly question, but some companies, like Viator, are actually aggregators – meaning they sell other companies' experiences, rather than provide their own. The problem with this, of course, is that then there's no real way to do much research on the guides or company you'll actually get, since the company name isn't revealed on the aggregator site until after you have booked.

2) Is this a walking tour or a driving tour?

Many of the top tour companies on Tripadvisor are for driver-guides. While there are obvious benefits to a driving tour, particularly for people with mobility issues, keep in mind that it probably won't involve an in-depth exploration of sights like the Forum or Colosseum, which you have to explore on foot. And even the most nimble of driver-guides may not be able to get you right next to some sites – like the Trevi Fountain, which is surrounded by a pedestrian area.

3) What are some keywords that pop up the most often in people's reviews about this company's guides?

"Enthusiasm"? "Expertise"? "Insider's tips"? "Academic"? Whatever adjectives they are, make sure that kind of personality fits with what you're looking for. (And yes, different tour companies have a particular "brand" – and therefore type of tour-guide style – that they go for).

4) How dependable does the company seem?

Do any reviews point out not getting the tour they were promised, or experiencing something like hidden fees or long lines?

5) How does the company respond to criticism?

If they did make a mistake, do they address it, and do they adequately respond to the customer's complaint?

6) What is the maximum group size?

In general, anything smaller than 15 feels fairly intimate and personal. Much larger than that, especially larger than 30, and you're getting into cruise-group-tour territory.

7) What exactly is included in my purchase?

Some companies include all your ticket fees in the cost of the tour; some don't. Make sure you won't be surprised by any "hidden fees" on the day of.

8) Will I be entering every sight listed on the itinerary,

or just walking by it?

This is a big one! If you read a description too quickly, you might think you're entering a sight with a guide, when you're not. (I've had several consulting clients over the years, for example, who believed that their tours of the Vatican *did* include St. Peter's Basilica; when we double-checked, it turned out that, sure enough, the tours stopped at the *entrance* to St. Peter's instead).

Finally, familiarize yourself with the company's cancellation policy. And make sure to print out any meeting point instructions, maps, and contact numbers before you head to Rome.

What about booking restaurants?

You're no doubt already aware that, if you'd like to have a blow-out or special occasion dinner at one of Rome's fancier spots, you'll need to book reservations in advance. What tends to come as more of a surprise to people is that even for many of Rome's more down-home spots, it can be even *more* important to book in advance. But it makes sense: While people head to a spot like La Pergola only for a very special occasion, Rome's most beloved trattorias are popular for anyone, any time, any night. You also could argue that, because so many of the restaurants in Rome's center are, contrary to stereotype, incredibly overpriced and mediocre, the few good ones which are left wind up fielding all of the bookings. Plus, thanks to the Roman penchant for two or three-hour dinners, restaurants tend to plan for just two table seatings – generally, one between 8pm and 9pm, and a later one at 10pm or 10:30pm – which means they can book up surprisingly quickly.

For that reason, if you have your heart set on trying a particular restaurant, make a reservation. That's all the more true if there's only one night, or one time, that you can make it, and becomes doubly true if you're not just a couple, but a group.

That doesn't tend to come as welcome news to my clients, who generally have an idea (and who doesn't?) of being able to wander around cobblestoned streets, pick a lovely spot at random when the mood strikes, and sit down to a fantastic, authentic, good-value meal. In fact, I've found that one of the most enduring stereotypes about Italy is that you can eat anywhere and eat well. The reality, I'm afraid, is quite different in Rome, as it is in other Italian cities like Florence and Venice. It isn't just Italy, of course. Would you expect to be able to do the same in Paris around the Louvre, or New York around Times Square? Probably not. Rome – particularly around major sites like the Spanish Steps, Piazza Navona or the Colosseum – is the same. And, just like those other cities, if you want to enjoy the best (and best-value) food that Rome has to offer, you do need to do a bit of research… and, particularly for the most popular places in the historic center, and definitely if you're a group, book at least a few days in advance.

How far you take this, of course, is up to you. If you're a "foodie" (read: You've been dreaming about the perfect *carbonara* or gelato since booking this trip, and one mediocre dinner could ruin your week), then I'd suggest that you do as much planning around where to eat as you do around what to see. I have a few suggestions later which you should read now; you might also want to check out recommendations from two of my favorite food writers, Katie Parla (p a r l a f o o d . c o m) and E l i z a b e t h   M i n c h i l l i (elizabethminchilliinrome.com). I'd also strongly suggest that you spend the €10 or €15 to load up a Skype account with enough international calling credit to call abroad and make bookings, especially for dinners, where online booking isn't available (that's most places).

If you enjoy good food but it's still well below seeing the Colosseum and the Sistine Chapel on your priority list, then take a slightly more laid-back approach. Do some research about where, ideally, you'd like to eat. For one or two of your must-eat spots (if you have any), particularly for dinners, book where you can online or via email. If you have others, wait until you arrive in Rome and try to make reservations then, either by calling if you have a local SIM or by asking your hotel to do it for you – keeping in mind that there's a chance, at the point, you might not get the day or time you wanted. For the rest of your meals, have some places in mind, but take the chance when you get a good gut feeling about a place (and report back to me with any new finds, please!).

Finally, although I note in the restaurants section where I'd strongly recommend reservations, some popular places that tend to fill up especially far (i.e. at least a week) in advance include Roscioli, Cesare al Casaletto and Flavio al Velavevodetto.

Do I need to speak Italian?

From first-time visitors to Rome, one of the questions I get most frequently is how much Italian is needed to get around.

For the most part, if you're planning on doing what 99.9% of travelers to Rome do – namely, seeing the major sites and eating out in the center – then the answer is simple: None. Rome sees 9 million tourists per year (many of them English speakers); particularly in the center, the city is full of people who work with tourists on a daily basis. That means you can assume that most people there will have basic English comprehension.

But just because we *can* assume that, of course, doesn't mean we should.

The biggest caveat to the "you'll be fine without the local language" argument goes for anywhere in the world, not just Italy. If you've traveled abroad before, you've probably already experienced how people anywhere appreciate when you speak a few words of their language. On the other hand, few things are more abrasive than someone who walks into a restaurant or shop in a foreign country and, without so much as a "Do you speak English?"-type preamble in the local language, launches into their own tongue.

The second caveat is that, if you have time to get beyond the most basic *"Ciao!"*, *"Grazie"* and *"Arrivederci"*, having a grasp of other vocabulary will help on a day-to-day level. You'll be able to tell the entrance from the exit from the toilet (and the men's restroom from the women's). You'll be able to not only ask someone on the street for directions, but understand their answer (always the more difficult part). And, while it may sound trivial, you'll truly be able to read menus better. Although English translations are nearly universal at restaurants in Rome now, that doesn't mean that the translations are very good – particular favorites include *spaghetti alle vongole veraci* (spaghetti with a particular kind of small baby clam) as "spaghetti of the voracious clams" and *crocchette di palate* (potato croquettes) as "shaken dicks"... I kid you not.

Make a step further into an intermediate or advanced grasp of Italian, meanwhile, and whole world of being able to converse with people in *their* language opens up to you. Obviously, many would argue that, in some ways, that's the whole point of travel: It allows you to truly begin to understand the local culture you've come here to explore.

The third caveat is that, even in the center of Rome, you may find yourself interacting with someone with very little English – a taxi driver, say, or a owner of an off-the-beaten-track mom-and-pop store. It's relatively unlikely, but of course it can happen. Those odds get a lot higher when you leave the city center, or the city altogether.

And finally, even if you're a beginning Italian speaker, practicing your language skills in Italy is a pleasant experience – and not just because it's always more fun to use Italian while ordering *un bicchiere di vino rosso della casa* or buying *due biglietti per il treno a Firenze* in Italy than when you're pretending to do those things in a faraway classroom. It's also fun because most Italians will let you muddle through it. You may have experienced how in some places, if you start to speak the local language poorly, someone will respond to you with quick, often flawless English (whether that's to put you out of your misery or show off their own language skills is up to interpretation). Not so here. When I first moved to Rome and spoke Italian like a toddler (but one with a strong American accent), everyone – waiters, bartenders, the cobbler, the handyman – let me. We would carry on entire half-hour long conversations in which they probably understood one out of every four ideas I was trying to convey. It was only months later that I found out nearly all of them spoke proficient English.

Rather than feel annoyed, I found it endearing: they were patient enough to let me try. That makes speaking Italian in Italy pretty rewarding – as long as you have a high tolerance for humiliation, at least.

That being said, you don't *have* to do any of these things. If you walk into a store and immediately ask "*Parla inglese?*", it's more than likely someone will not only speak enough English to communicate with you, but will be gracious about it. But because of the number of foreigners visiting, these locals often don't have a choice about speaking at least some English. You, on the other hand, do have a choice about speaking some Italian.

Do I need to rent a car?

When I started this section, part of me was tempted to keep it short and, literally, just write "no". But, as ever, it's slightly more complicated.

Here, though, is the simple part: You don't need a car for the days when you're in Rome. In fact – because of the traffic, lack of parking, zaniness of road etiquette and the fact that Rome is both a very walkable city and one relatively well-connected by public transport, especially by buses – having a car would be a liability, an expense, and a headache.

You also don't need a car for your trip to Italy at all if you're visiting only cities (like Rome, Naples, Florence, Milan and Venice) or cities interspersed with day trips (most of which will be accessible via public transport, though, of course, check before you plan). In fact, the only times I recommend driving in Italy are if you're planning to stay in the countryside or in smaller towns, or – only maybe – if you're a family of four or five and it turns out to be far more economical to hire a car than to buy separate train tickets. But driving in Italy could be a whole book in itself.

So I'll still keep this rather short: Avoid having a car in Rome.

Should I book a transfer?

If you know you will have a hard time managing your luggage

on your own or you are traveling as a group of more than four people, then you may want to book a private transfer to pick you up on your arrival at the airport. When I say "have a hard time managing your luggage", I mean for the entire trip from the airport to your hotel – which, if you go by public transport, may include not only a train into the city center, but a metro or bus from there. Not all metro stations have escalators or elevators (the Colosseum stop doesn't, for example), and those that do can't always be relied upon. (Plus, if you're coming in summer, don't underestimate how hot those stations and the metro and buses can get).

If you know you won't want to start your trip that way, one option, which you would have to book in advance, is a private transfer. This is often a slightly more expensive option than a taxi, and, of course, much more expensive than public transport. As you might expect, it is also the most hassle-free option (assuming you book with a reliable transfer company; always check Tripadvisor for the latest reviews).

If you are flying into Fiumicino, which you likely will be if you're coming from outside of Europe, you don't have to book your transport in advance. You also can take a taxi from the taxi stand outside of arrivals. In that case, you may have to wait for a larger van if you are a group of four to six people plus luggage (or take two vehicles separately). The taxis here are relatively trustworthy, and each vehicle should cost €48 for the trip into the Rome center. (More on this later).

However, if your flight is into Ciampino (which it will be if it is with Ryanair, EasyJet or one of the other budget European airlines) and you know you have too much luggage, or too large of a group, to hassle with public transport or a bus, then *definitely* book a transfer (or consider Uber). Do not use the taxis here.

You can also use Uber from either airport, which can be a good alternative if you want to decide when you arrive, rather than book a transfer. But Uber's situation has been precarious lately, so make sure it's still legal and running right before your trip.

If you know convenience will be key for you, though, and

you're not a tight budget (or willing to pay for the case at the start of your trip), and you don't feel like fiddling with the Uber app on arrival, then do book a transfer in advance. There are a million and one companies which offer this (and many tour companies do, as well), so don't feel you need to go with the one that your hotel offers; do a little research online and check recent reviews instead.

The good news is these, unlike the Borghese Gallery or even some popular restaurants, usually can be booked just a day or two in advance – so don't panic if you've left it relatively last-minute.

The essentials: Your phone and your bank

At least a couple of days in advance of your trip, there are two last things you'll want to sort: Your phone and your money.

Setting up your smartphone or tablet to go abroad

This is one of those things that's changed a lot since I first wrote this book in 2012. Back then, even as a full-time blogger and travel journalist, I had a Nokia brick phone – one of those amazingly sturdy little blocks that could call, text and, most importantly, survive any number of situations, from a week without being recharged to falling onto the pavement. (Oops). Now, nearly everyone has a smart phone.

When it comes to traveling, of course, that makes it much easier. No longer do you get lost on your way to the Vatican museums or dinner reservation; just pull up Google Maps. No longer do you have to jot down notes from websites or books; now, you have them in your pocket. No longer do you have to wait to show your loved ones what a wonderful trip you're having; now, they can watch every frame of your Trevi Fountain coin throw in real-time!

But as you know if you've traveled internationally before, that doesn't mean traveling with a smart phone (or tablet) is simple.

For one thing, of course, there's the issue of connection. While some European cities are almost completely covered by a wifi network, Rome is a little bit behind in that regard. There are "open" wifi hotspots scattered here and there which you'll see pop up on your phone – but you need an Italian mobile phone number to authenticate them.

Fortunately, most hotels these days do offer wifi. (Oddly, it tends to be only the most expensive, five-star hotels that charge extra; for nearly everywhere else, it's free). Some restaurants and cafes will, as well. But if you're planning on using your phone fairly regularly – or just want to have the option to – then you'll need to have access to the 3G or 4G network.

There are a couple of ways to do this. The first is for those who have an unlocked phone. Americans are at a disadvantage here; in most of the rest of the world, phones can be unlocked and the SIM card traded without a problem, but not, unfortunately, for a US mobile. If you have a phone that can be unlocked, you're probably already familiar with how easy it is to swap out a SIM. In which case (depending, of course, on where you're from and what your data plan is; within the European Union, for example, you can use a phone in any country without an extra charge) you'll just have to walk into a store once you're in Rome to buy a new one. You don't need a long-term contract to get a new SIM in Italy – just make sure you sign up for one of the "pay-as-you-go" packages instead.

Since you can't throw a gelato in Rome without hitting a Vodafone, Wind, TIM or Tre, finding a mobile phone shop to help you out won't be hard. (Do make sure you bring your passport or EU I.D. with you, though, as it's required by law in order to purchase a new SIM). Figuring out the difference between their plans and what will work best for you can be the trickier part, so I'd recommend doing a little bit of research online in advance.

If you're stuck with a US phone that can't be unlocked, first, check to make sure it will work in Italy, anyway. (Most do). To do this, just see if your phone supports GSM 900 and GSM 1800 frequencies. Assuming it does, you can either jailbreak it (which is complicated and not recommended) in order to unlock it. More likely, though, you'll probably want to go with a data plan instead. Make sure to give your provider a call (it's probably best to inform yourself of the various options on their website first) to figure out a package that works best for you.

If you have a tablet, check that, too. Most iPads are sold unlocked, even in the US.

Or, of course, you could forgo 24/7 connectivity for a few days. Some would say that's the real vacation!

Call your bank and credit card companies

Particularly if you don't do much travel abroad, you'll want to call your bank and credit card companies to have them make a note that you'll be in Italy. There's always the chance that, on your first international transaction in a while, they might shut down your accounts for security reasons. Not something you want to have to deal with.

While we're on the topic of money, by the way: Please don't plan to use traveler's cheques while you're abroad; they're unwieldy and a nuisance. And (of course) don't bring a pile of cash from home to change into euros when you arrive, which isn't just unsafe, but inevitably will get you stung with high fees and a terrible exchange rate. Instead, bring your bank card and, when in Rome, look for any "bancomat". Even though you'll have €5 to €10 of fees per transaction, the fact that it's the best exchange rate you'll get makes up for it.

What should I plan to wear?

One question clients often ask me is what to wear during a trip to Italy. There's something about *la bella figura* that intimidates even the savviest world travelers into second-guessing their sartorial choices.

This isn't unreasonable. Particularly in the upmarket areas of Rome's *centro storico*, both Italian women and men have a kind of dress code that sets them apart from other nationalities. (I have gotten surprisingly good at watching passersby and, by what they're wearing alone, pinpointing whether they're Italian, German, American, Spanish – you name it). One part of this "code" is that it is, indeed, slightly dressier than some other cultures. It's rare, for example, that you'll see a man wearing blue jeans to dinner, practically unfathomable to have on tennis shoes. And while Italian women hardly live in dresses and heels, there is that extra "something" – whether just a tad more jewelry or perfectly applied eyeliner – that often sets them apart.

Of course, as for any cultural generality, this isn't true across the board. And one of the most interesting things I've noticed about fashion in Rome over the years is how the under-25 set, in particular, has wholly embraced American street style: nothing seems to be cooler than Nike sneakers, jeans and sweatshirts. But if you're watching locals, rather than visitors, you probably will notice a different (and, depending on where you're from, possibly slightly more "elegant") kind of dress than what you see back home.

Does this mean I'm advocating every traveler to Rome ditch their comfortable shoes and jeans to sightsee? Absolutely not. For one thing, no matter how much you try to mimic local dress, people will know you're a visitor – whether because of accessories, a haircut, hand gestures or, of course, the language you're speaking. You'll never completely blend in. (I still don't). Secondly, nor should you. Being respectful of the local culture – i.e., by not showing up to dinner in sweatpants – is important. But so is your comfort and practicality.

Since you've gotten this far, though, you're probably interested in experiencing Rome as the locals do, and some of the fun of that can be in how you dress. But even more importantly, even if you'll never be mistaken for a local by dressing in a certain way, what you can do is show that you're not a first-time tourist. That makes you a less likely target for nefarious types (whether that be dishonest taxi drivers, waiters or even pickpockets) who tend to find their easiest prey is first-time travelers.

Want to know how to tweak your wardrobe? You probably already know to ditch the sweatshirt, the fanny pack (or "bum bag", for British readers), the white socks and white tennis shoes (unless you're 21 and they're Nike Airs). Other things to consider are that, even in the heat of summer, Romans will rarely walk around the city in short shorts and tiny tank tops (consider an airy sundress or skirt instead); it's less common for men to wear shorts at all, but particularly in the evenings; and any time of year, leather or suede shoes — whether ballerina flats, boots, loafers or even shoes shaped similarly to tennis shoes — are usually preferable to athletic sneakers. That being said, if you're planning on doing as the (over-25) locals do, make sure that any shoes you're planning on walking around with are broken in. No matter how comfortable those ballerina flats seem to look, you just won't know until you've been walking around in them for four hours, or more, at a stretch.

Again, remember: You don't have to do any of this. If you know the only way you can handle so much walking on cobblestones is in your favorite pair of athletic sneakers, don't hesitate to wear them. The most important thing is that you're comfortable.

What else should I pack?

Clothing aside, other than European plug adapters (and power converters, if you're planning to bring a heat-emitting device like a hairdryer or straighter), here are some items which you might *not* have thought of:

•*Student I.D.:* If you're a university student (or someone else you're traveling with is), don't forget a student I.D.! You'll save significantly at sights like the Vatican (where the reduced price is €8 instead of €16), and can come in handy elsewhere, too.

•*European I.D.:* If you're an E.U. citizen, make sure to bring an I.D. with you whenever you're sightseeing. Young Europeans (under 25), teachers, and sometimes the over-65 set get discounts at many of Rome's sites.

•*Document of academic affiliation:* If you're an undergraduate or graduate student, postdoc, Ph.D. or teacher of a faculty that is either architecture, cultural heritage, education, or a humanities discipline like archaeology or art history, even as a non-European, you should be able to get free entry to state-run sites and museums (such as the Colosseum) by showing a certificate of enrollment or valid faculty document for the current academic year.

•*Backpack:* I don't recommend sightseeing with a backpack. It's hot, easy to pickpocket, marks you as a tourist, and, generally, unnecessary. For security reasons, it's also now forbidden to have at the Colosseum (so make sure you don't have it on you that day!). However, it can come in handy at the *end* of your trip: When all of those souvenirs you've bought make it impossible to close your checked bag, just pop the extra into your backpack and make it your new carry-on.

•*Earplugs:* Not sure if your apartment, B&B, or hotel has double-glazed windows? Then don't be without a pair.

•*Pack of tissues and hand sanitizer:* We'll talk about where to find toilets in Rome later, but for now, note that not every bathroom is as well-stocked as you might like. Generally speaking, it's a good idea to have a pack of tissues and a little bottle of hand sanitizer on you, just in case.

•*Shawl or cardigan, even in summer:* If you're packing skin-bearing summer outfits, this is a must. It's respectful to cover your shoulders and knees in every church in Italy, and some, including St. Peter's Basilica, won't allow you in otherwise.

•*Money belt:* No, this is not a must. In fact, I've never carried one around myself. But, yes, there is pickpocketing in Rome (more on that later), and particularly if you don't trust yourself to be aware of what's going on around you at all times, it can be a good option.

Get excited

You're almost there! You've booked your flight and your hotel (or B&B, or apartment, or convent). You've figured out how you're going to avoid the lines at Rome's top sights. Maybe you've even booked a tour or two. Most of your trip's essentials are nailed down.

Which means it's time to... get excited. It's not exactly rocket science, but one way I always like to gear up for a trip is by doing little reading – or even movie-watching – about the place I'm going. Luckily, for Rome, there are hundreds of options. Here are just a few of my favorites:

Nonfiction books (that you'll forget are nonfiction)

Although I am, admittedly, a history nerd, even I find it hard to choke down dense, academic tomes. As a child, I loved historical fiction. As an adult, I've been thrilled to find books that are every bit as engrossing – but where everything in them is factual, so I don't have to wonder which part the author imagined versus what actually happened. (Though, of course, that can be equally rewarding).

Here are some of my recent favorites, if you'd like some recommendations...

There have been countless dramatized versions of how the Sistine Chapel came to be painted, but it's hard to beat Ross King's nonfictional, but written-like-a-novel *Michelangelo and the Pope's Ceiling*. King is the guy who wrote *Brunelleschi's Dome* – also a recommendation (especially if you're heading to Florence). And he has a knack for narrative that will have you hanging on every twist and turn in the Sistine Chapel saga.

Jonathan Harr's *The Lost Painting* is so fast-paced, it's easy to forget it's not a detective thriller. The book tells the story of how, in 1992, a young art student tracked down one of the world's great, missing masterpieces: Caravaggio's *The Taking of the Christ*, which had been gone for more than 200 years. Think the *Da Vinci Code*, only well-written and nonfiction.

If you've seen the film *Monuments Men*, you already know some of this story: How the Allies sent a team of art historians to Europe to try to save its art from Nazi devastation. But whereas I wasn't a big fan of the film, I could barely put down the book *Saving Italy* (which, of course, is focused on the hair-raising activities they undertook across the peninsula), written by the same author. I'm pretty sure that I kept saying "Oh my God, did you know this?" to my other half so often while reading the book, he couldn't wait for me to be finished. I promise, once you know the stories of what Italy's art and architecture has been through, you'll see the cityscape and art of Rome (and Florence, and Milan, and…) in a completely new way.

In *Cleopatra: A Life*, Stacy Schiff gave herself a tough task: Resetting the reputation of someone when the only information we have is from her enemies. She does a commendable job, and the result is an addictive biography. You know how it all ends, but you can't help turning the page for more about this confident, extraordinary, anything-but-promiscuous woman Schiff paints. Plus, while most of the book deals with Alexandria, its section on what Rome would have looked like to Cleopatra on her visit (in brief: a backwater) is pretty entertaining.

R. A. Scott has been slammed for some historical inaccuracies in *Basilica: The Splendor and the Scandal: Building St. Peter's*, but she deserves major kudos for telling the sweeping 200-year history of the "new" St. Peter's Basilica with both page-turning speed and colorful details (Michelangelo didn't just "make his escape"; he made it "wrapped in a lavender cloak the color of dusk, riding headlong against a sharp north wind"). The enormity of the basilica, and its history, is compacted into 300 quick-read pages. That's a downside if you plan to be the next big St. Peter's Basilica expert… but a positive if you don't want your head to hurt.

It's too bad that the title of Christopher Hibbert's *The Borgias and Their Enemies: 1431-1519* is so dry, because the content is anything but; I devoured it like a beach read. In case you're not familiar with them (or the television show), the Borgias were essentially the most bloodthirsty, morally dubious clan in the papacy's history – and that's saying something. After all, the only thing that makes a story about a ridiculously dysfunctional family even more fun… is when it's true!

I'm cheating a little bit by including this book, because you wouldn't, in fact, mistake it for a novel. But if you're interested in the history of ancient Rome – all of it, from Romulus and Remus up to the empire's "fall" – then Mary Beard's new book *SPQR* is your best bet, even if you've never studied it before. Beard treats you like you're a smart person who probably has heard of the story of Romulus and Remus, but might need your memory jogged, just in case… and who definitely is curious about how that story came to be and what on earth all that fratricide really meant. And she's candid and clear-eyed not only about what's true and what's not, but also what the Romans were really like (she dispatches one ancient legend with a simple "This is another case of Roman exaggeration"). The *New York Times* called her approach "a crisp and merciless clarity". It's also one that makes a very complicated subject very, very readable.

Okay, this one's a cheat too. But it's just so good. In many ways, this is basically the book that, in my dream of dreams, I wanted to write – except there's no way I could have done it as well as veteran Roman journalist Corrado Augias. His *The Secrets of Rome* is a well-researched, beautifully-written journey that leapfrogs around 2,700 years of Roman history. Each chapter takes a different corner of the city as the jumping-off point for a fascinating tale. Some are little-known, but even the stories that are famous – like Caesar's assassination – have parts that will surprise anyone but a Roman history PhD. Because of its richness of local details, this is best if you've been to Rome before – or as something to thumb through once you're there for the first time.

Novels (which will set the mood)

When it comes to Rome, I tend to go for history. But if fiction is your preference, of course, there is fantastic literature about (or based in) the city that can help whet your appetite just as much.

Here are just five to get you started.

Tennessee Williams' very first novel was *The Roman Spring of Mrs. Stone*, which follows a washed-up, wealthy American widow through a romantic entanglement with a younger man in gritty post-war Rome.

For another glimpse of Rome in the same time period (and even bleaker – consider it your *Eat, Pray, Love* antidote), *The Ragazzi*, by venerated filmmaker Pier Paolo Pasolini, is a novel about life for a young boy growing up in Rome's postwar slums (now the more-than-respectable neighborhood of Monteverde).

If you're a fan of sprawling sagas, the *Masters of Rome* series by Colleen McCullough (of *The Thorn Birds* fame) isn't high literature, but will keep you captivated – through all seven books that take you from 110 B.C. to the final years of the Roman Republic, if you're committed.

Gore Vidal's bestselling novel *Julian* takes on a period of Roman history that's gone remarkably undramatized: The last years of the empire, specifically the 4th century. As the title would imply, it's the story of Julian – a philosopher, military genius and emperor who tried to fight the spread of Christianity that was destabilizing the empire, and who was murdered at just 32 years old.

Of course, though, if you're interested in the Roman Empire, Robert Graves' *I, Claudius* – written as a colorful autobiography from the emperor's perspective – is a classic for a reason.

Prefer it with popcorn?

If you're not a big reader, no problem. (And thanks for getting through this book!). There are plenty of other ways to get your Rome fix.

Many of the above books, of course, have been turned into movies, including *I, Claudius* and *The Roman Spring of Mrs. Stone* (there's also an earlier film with Vivien Leigh, if you can find it anywhere). And then there are the classics, like *Roman Holiday, Three Coins in the Fountain* and, of course, Federico Fellini's (much-misunderstood – the name is ironic, people!) *La Dolce Vita.*

If you just want to watch a movie with some beautiful Rome backdrops to get a sense of the sights you'll see, you could do worse than *Only You, The Talented Mr. Ripley* or, fine, *Eat, Pray, Love* (a book and movie I generally avoid mentioning, thanks to just how much it's contributed to sickening-sweet stereotypes about life in Italy). For something far grittier, check out the classic film *Bicycle Thieves,* about (are you seeing a theme here yet?) life in postwar Rome.

The number of sumptuous Rome-set television shows that have aired in the past few years, meanwhile, could keep you busy for hours: *Rome*, *The Borgias* and the latest showstopper, *The Young Pope*, which imagines Jude Law as a radical new head of the Church. There's also the less-sumptuous, but gripping and gritty, new Netflix series *Suburra*, which delves into the contemporary world of organized crime.

You can also...

•*Download lectures* on Roman history and Renaissance art (for free!) from iTunes University

•*Subscribe to podcasts* on a topic that interests you (some of my favorites are "The History of Rome" and "Classical Mythology Podcast")

•*Watch documentaries* from the History Channel or National Geographic Channel, or stream them on Netflix or Amazon.

Chapter 3
En Route to Rome

Getting Around

You're on your way! (Or almost). But now that you're en route, how will you get from your airport to Rome? And how will you get *around* Rome?

In this section, I'll walk you through the most important tips and tricks to transport in Rome (…no pun intended), including how to handle the train station, how to get to Rome from the airport, why you should never take at taxi from Ciampino, how to take taxis elsewhere in Rome (without getting ripped off) and how to use public transportation.

Arriving by train

If you're taking a train from one city to another in Italy, getting the ticket can be the easy part. Navigating the station itself can be trickier. Here is what to know. (If you're arriving via flight, skip to the next section instead).

First, once you've gotten your ticket and are at the station, look for a big, hanging board with all of the newest trains listed. (One dead giveaway for where this is tends to be the crowd of people standing underneath it!). Don't panic if, at first glance, your train isn't there. You might be too early, since only the soonest departures will be listed. Or you might be looking at "Arrivi" (arrivals) rather than "Partenze" (departures). It's also often easiest to go by the train's *number* and departure time, rather than your particular destination, because trains are listed by their final destination – your destination may not be on the board at all. (You can find this either when you book it, or on your ticket itself; it'll say "TRENO" followed by the number).

Once you've found your train, look where it says "BIN," for "binario" (platform). That's your platform number. Don't worry if this takes a while to come up – you won't be the only one hurrying to the train, and it's rare for a conductor to leave a crowd behind on the platform!

Before boarding, don't forget to validate your ticket. You don't have to do this for fast trains that required a reservation–but if you're uncertain, it's always best to be on the safe side. The validation machines tend to be all over the station, as well as on the platform; they're usually yellow. To stamp, put your ticket in the slot, arrows facing in, and push until you hear the stamp. If you don't do this and you were supposed to, you can get a heavy fine when (or if) your ticket is checked.

Depending on what kind of train you booked, check your ticket for your seat. After the train number, it might say "Carrozza" followed by a number. That's your carriage number. Then it will say "posti", which lists your seat number. Many Italian trains have reserved seats, so make sure you sit in the right one. Even if there are a ton of empty seats elsewhere, you never know how many people might be getting on, and trying to sit in their reserved seats, at a later stop. (If someone's in your seat, showing them your ticket will usually suffice for them to move).

Once that's all behind you, you can relax. Just don't forget where you put your ticket, as it may be checked by the conductor (you can get a stiff fine if you're found riding without a ticket!). Also be aware of those around you: Both train stations and trains themselves are a favorite haunt for pickpockets, particularly on the major lines, like from Naples to Rome. Know where your things are at all times, be careful of putting your bag or purse on the ground where you can't see it, and never fall asleep with your purse next to you if you're traveling alone. Other than that, look out the window and enjoy the ride.

How to get to Rome from the airport

You've landed in Italy, and you can't wait to get to Rome and start exploring! The good news: You're almost there.

If you read the last chapter, then you know that one relatively ease-free way to get into the center is with a private transfer, which needs to be booked in advance. Here are your other options.

From Fiumicino-Leonardo da Vinci airport

If you're flying in from abroad, you'll probably be coming into Fiumicino (FCO), Rome's international airport. If you haven't booked a transfer in advance, then from there, you have three options: Train, bus, or cab.

Train

The train station at Fiumicino is located within short walking distance of the baggage claim. Just follow the signs for the train station, or ask anyone at the airport.

There are two trains that run from the train station:

•The Regionale (local) train: This goes directly from the airport to several stations in the center. The most useful for you, if you're staying in the historic center, will probably be Ostiense station. To get from there to the center, you would follow the signs for the metro; a 5-minute walk brings you to the Piramide metro stop on the B line. From there, it's two stops to the Colosseo metro stop or four to Termini, where you can switch to the A line. This is the train that commuters use. The cost is €8 each way, and the ride takes a half an hour. If you're staying in Testaccio or near the

Colosseum, don't want to deal with road traffic, and/or are on a tight budget, this is a good bet.

•The Leonardo da Vinci Express ("tourist") train: This train is geared towards Rome's visitors. Unsurprisingly, therefore, it costs more (€14 each way). It goes directly from the airport to Termini station, making no stops, and takes a half an hour. However, because it does go to Termini, unlike the other train, then if you know you need to take the metro line A to your hotel, this may make your overall journey a bit shorter.

Bus

There are also several buses that run from Fiumicino to the city center. They take a little under an hour, depending on traffic, but are a cheaper option than the train. They include the SIT bus shuttle (sitbusshuttle.com), Terravision bus (run by Ryanair, terravision.eu), COTRAL bus (cotralspa.it), and ATRAL-Lazio bus (atral-lazio.com), and each cost about €5, each way. Check websites for the exact departure times and prices.

Cab

There is a flat rate to go from the Fiumicino airport to the city center: €48, including all luggage and any extra charges. As soon as you get in a taxi at the airport, therefore, make sure your driver does not run the meter and only pay that amount at the end. It is illegal for your driver to charge you more. (Find out more on how to take taxis in Rome later).

By the center of Rome, by the way, I (and the city of Rome) mean anything within the Aurelian walls I mentioned when talking about hotels. That includes the heart of Rome, plus Trastevere and the Vatican neighborhood. In other words, if you're staying anywhere near Piazza Navona, the Spanish Steps, St. Peter's, Termini, or the Colosseum, you're good – which I expect will cover 99% of the people reading this book. If you have any doubt about whether the hotel is in the *centro storico*, ask your hotel in advance; if it's outside of the historic center, your driver has the right to run the meter and to charge you supplements instead of the flat fare.

Uber

At least for now, the app taking over the world's cities has made it to Rome (much to the consternation of taxi drivers). That "at least for now" is an important caveat. The powers that be already have yanked Uber once, only to have the rule overturned. As of November 2017, it's operating again, but as this could change at any time, make sure you check before you rely on it.

Assuming it is still operating, the basic idea of this ride-sharing app is similar to other cities. But there's one big difference. Rome doesn't offer UberX or the other lower-priced services; it only has the higher-end services: UberBLACK, UberLUX and UberVAN. That means that, often, taking an Uber is as expensive as (or more expensive than) taking a taxi. But it also means that drivers often aren't "normal" people picking up some cash on the side, but rather professional drivers, which is a benefit.

From Fiumicino airport (which has wifi, so you can book an Uber using the Uber app on your phone when you arrive), it should be about €40 into the center, although, as always with Uber, it depends on pricing and availability at that time. (You get a fare estimate before you book).

From Ciampino airport

Flying in from another airport in Europe? Especially if you're taking a budget airline, then you'll likely land at Ciampino (CIA). Although it can seem like Ciampino is less convenient than Fiumicino, as there's no train station directly there, it's actually even faster and cheaper to connect to Rome from than Fiumicino. If you haven't booked a transfer in advance, then from there, you have several options. Your cheapest options are the train, bus, or metro; for private options, you can also take a taxi (but don't – more later on why), private transfer, or Uber.

Train

The good news: There is a train station at Ciampino. The not-as-good news: It's not right at the airport. To get there, you have to take one of the ATRAL or COTRAL buses from the airport. The ATRAL buses depart roughly every 40 minutes (full schedule at atral-lazio.com), while the COTRAL leaves between every 10 and 40 minutes (more information at cotralspa.it). The ATRAL costs €1.20, plus an extra €1.20 per piece of luggage, while the COTRAL costs €1.10. While that makes the COTRAL seem better, note that you can buy ATRAL tickets right at Ciampino airport in the arrivals area or directly on the bus, while COTRAL isn't sold at the airport, but rather from tobacco shops and other sales points outside the airport.

The drive to the train station takes 5 minutes. From there, the train to Rome's Termini train station departs about every 8-10 minutes, takes 15 minutes and costs just €1.50.

If you time it right, this can be the fastest way to get to Rome's center, as well as the cheapest. But if you have a lot of luggage, or just want to have as few transport legs as possible, I'd go with the next option – a direct bus – instead.

Bus

For most people, the bus from Ciampino to Rome is the most convenient, still budget-friendly option. Two buses run directly from the Ciampino airport into the Rome center: the SIT bus (sitbusshuttle.com) and Terravision (terravision.eu). Prices are €5 one-way or €9 round-trip with SIT or €4 one-way and €8 round-trip with Terravision, and the ride takes a half an hour to 45 minutes, depending on traffic. Both have just one stop, Rome's Termini train station, so you don't have to worry about missing your stop. From Termini, you can take a bus or metro (line A or B) to your final destination.

Figuring these buses out couldn't really be much easier: When you exit the baggage claim at Ciampino, you'll see the kiosks advertising them right in front of you. Just walk up and ask when the next one is leaving (I recommend asking at both, so you can buy your ticket for the one leaving first!). You can buy your ticket right there – no need to reserve in advance – and they'll direct you to where exactly the bus is.

Metro

This is only worth considering if you're staying at accommodation in San Giovanni or the Esquiline (or somewhere else close to a stop on Rome's metro line A, but before Termini). You can take a bus from the airport to the Anagnina metro station, which is on line A. The bus leaves every 30 to 40 minutes, takes about 15 minutes and costs €1.20, plus an extra €1.20 per piece of luggage. From Anagnina, the metro (which costs €1.50) leaves every couple of minutes and arrives at San Giovanni station in 15 minutes, Manzoni (Esquiline) in 17 and Termini station in 20 minutes.

Cab

I'm including this because, yes, it is an option. And, technically, there is a flat rate set by the city to go from the Ciampino airport to the center of Rome, which includes the heart of Rome where most tourists stay, as well as the Vatican area and Trastevere. This price is €30, including all luggage and any extra charges. It's illegal for drivers to charge you more than this.

But, of course, they try to. Which is why, at least until the taxi drivers at Ciampino clean up their act, I don't recommend that anyone risks taking a cab from there.

Public transport not your thing? Even without a cab, you still have a couple of options.

Private transfer

There are dozens of companies in Rome offering private transfers, the benefit of which is − of course − it's convenient, you don't have to juggle your luggage and it takes the stress out of trying to navigate a new city's transport links. Of course, you have to pay for the privilege, as private transfers can be around €50 or more (the cost depends on number of passengers and amount of luggage). Do, however, make sure you book a reputable transfer company (among other things, double-check their recent reviews on a site like Tripadvisor); skip that step, and you run just as much risk of being ripped off as you would with a taxi (see below for more!).

Uber

As with FCO, Ciampino airport has wifi, so you can book an Uber using the Uber app on your phone when you arrive. (However, see my note for Fiumicino airport, above: Uber's situation can change in Rome at any time, so make sure it's legal and running before you leave). It should be about €40 into the center, although it depends on pricing and availability at that time. You get a fare estimate before you book.

Why you should never take a taxi from Ciampino

If you aren't flying into Ciampino, or you are but you've already definitively decided not to take a taxi, skip this section. Otherwise – or if you're just curious why I seem to keep berating the taxi drivers at Ciampino airport, in particular – I want to share a story.

The taxi drivers at Ciampino have a racket going on, and it revolves around (illegally) ripping off tourists.

Since I normally take the bus from Ciampino to the Rome center, for years, I had no idea. But then, after a 5-hour flight delay that meant I arrived to Ciampino exhausted (and harried), a friend and I decided to split a cab.

As you know from the previous section, a taxi from Ciampino airport to Rome is €30. That's the flat rate set by the city; it includes all passengers in the vehicle, all of their bags, and one stop in the center. It's illegal for drivers to charge more.

So, bags in hand, we walked out to the official taxi queue. Filled with registered, licensed, official taxis.

And, as is the case for all official taxis (to try to minimize the number of scams exactly like this one), each one had large lettering on the side saying that the flat rate, for Ciampino to Rome, is €30.

Here's where it potentially gets tricky: The writing directly on the cab calls the "Rome center" anything within the Aurelian walls of the city.

Of course, as a tourist, you wouldn't necessarily know what that means. But, as per how it is delineated in the city's laws, it includes the heart of Rome, plus Trastevere and the Vatican neighborhood. In other words, 99% of tourists coming into Ciampino (or Fiumicino) are staying within the walls, since it includes the area around the Spanish Steps, Termini train station, Piazza Navona, and St. Peter's are all in the center.

My friend and I lived right near the Colosseum, well within the walls.

The old (and sweet-looking! and smiley!) old taxi driver at the head of the queue went to take our bags. In Italian, we asked if there was any way he could do two stops – a favor, we knew, even though we live only 3 minutes apart from each other.

"*Sì, senza problema*," he said, putting our bags in his trunk. "I'll do both stops for €50."

"Oh, no, never mind," I said. "Forget it. We'll both just get dropped off at the same place, the Colosseum."

"Okay," he said. "I'll do that for €40."

Me: "What? It's €30."

Him: "No, it's €40."

Me (still in Italian): "Listen, I live in Rome. I know it's €30. That's the flat fare."

Him (taking my arm and pointing to the side of his cab): "No, but see, it's €30 to the walls of Rome. That's not where the Colosseum is."

Me (at this point, floored): "No, it's €30 to within the walls. To the center."

Him: "The Colosseum's not in the center."

(Um, we might have been wearing flip-flops, and I might have been speaking Italian with an American accent... but really?).

Taking my bag back from him, I turned to the other drivers. All of whom were loitering next to their cabs in a group, watching the exchange silently.

"So…" I said, flustered. "Will anyone here take us for, you know, the €30 flat fare?"

Crickets.

As I angrily dragged my bag toward the bus stop, along with my friend, another man appeared in the parking lot. "What happened?" he asked. I explained, briefly. "Look," he said, "I'm a taxi driver too, and I'll take you. Yes, for €30. Wait down the road."

As we headed a little bit down the street from the airport, I looked back. Sure enough, he'd gotten into another official, licensed taxi.

And the reason why he wanted to pick us up away from the others was clear: As he drove by them, they picked up on what he was doing and started – I kid you not – yelling at him and banging on his window.

All because… he was following the law.

Look, I should be used to stuff like this in Italy. But it had been a while since I've seen that blatant a display of law-flouting and intimidation; remember, again, these were all official taxi drivers. And watching them try to scare another driver into not following the law was something I won't forget for a while.

On top of that? How unfair to tourists! I had the good luck to know what the "center" and the "Aurelian walls" really mean. But not everyone does. And many visitors probably wonder how they wound up spending a ton of cash on what, in no traffic, can be as little as a 20-minute ride.

As the (legit) driver drove us home, he was apologetic for the others' behavior. "Look," he said, "they've been waiting out there for five hours without a single fare. That's why."

Right. And now, instead of getting a fare, they were going to sit and loiter in front of the airport for another few hours. Really smart.

The episode I outline above took place in 2013. That's a long time ago, and even in Rome, things change. Unfortunately, that doesn't seem to be one of them. As multiple recent posts on Tripadvisor point out, the same intimidation is still going on. And if they aren't cheating people with prices from the get-go, the drivers are figuring out other ways to run scams. As one person posted in October 2016: "We approached the taxi stand/driver and confirmed €30 to Trastevere as indicated on his door label (a white cab at stand just to the right outside of the arrivals door and Trastevere is inside the walls). We had even written our accommodation address down and presented it to the driver before getting into the car. Driver smiled, agreed "yes". However once loaded and we've taken off he tells us to "metro", as it's our first time in Rome we were confused but long story short, he dumped us at the nearest Underground (Anagnina metro station) and charged us €15 for the privilege. To top it off, in the shock and confusion I got out of the taxi and accidentally left my carry on bag in the vehicle. A check with the airport and even a follow up by our accommodation manager to the expected taxi company confirmed the driver didn't hand it into airport lost property (not that we really expected him too). Sorry to the honest taxi drivers out there but these guys are giving you and your city a bad name. My advice, AVOID TAXIS from Ciampino airport." I'd agree.

Public transportation in Rome

If I've scared you to death about taking a taxi in Rome (sorry!), then here's the good news. As much as Rome's residents complain about the city's public transportation, it tends to be much cleaner, more reliable, and better-connected than many visitors – at least those from the United States – are used to. And while, like any city transportation, Rome's bus and metro lines are easier to understand the longer you spend here, it's not impossible to get the hang of Rome's public transport in just a day or two.

Here's a quick guide to get you started.

How Rome's transport tickets work, and where to buy them

Rome's public transportation tickets combine access to the metro, buses, and trams. In other words, you don't buy one ticket for the bus and a separate ticket for the metro; a public transport ticket is a public transport ticket. Any individual ticket, therefore, costs €1.50 for 100 minutes of use, including one metro ride and *unlimited* bus and tram rides.

You can buy your ticket at the metro station before boarding your metro, and you can often (but not always) buy your ticket on the bus… but if you want to be super-sure you have a ticket on you (and you're not near a metro station), buy your ticket at a tobacco shop instead.

I can hear your "Huh?" from here. So allow me a quick aside…

The tobacco-transport connection

If you want to understand public transportation in Rome, or Rome in general, you have to understand… the tobacco shop.

In Italy, tobacco shops – marked by a sign hanging out their door with a big, impossible-to-miss "T" – don't just sell, you know, tobacco. They happen to be where you can pay a lot of your household bills. And buy phone credit. They also sell gum, postcards, notebooks, snacks… and metro and bus tickets. (They almost always have single tickets, and they normally have the multi-day passes you'll read about below, too; if not, the multi-day passes can be purchased at the ATAC ticket offices at Termini or at any of the metro stations).

The good news is that these tobacco shops are all over the city. So when you need to buy a ticket for the bus, the tobacco shop, or *tabaccaio* ("tah-bahk-AY-oh"), is what you should ask for. Inside, request a *biglietto per l'autobus* ("bill-yee-EHT-oh pear lot-oh-BOOS").

Should I buy a Roma Pass for unlimited public transport?

You can skip this if you've already read the section on sightseeing passes. If you haven't, now might be the time to look at it. But in short: Since the Roma Pass includes unlimited public transport, lots of travelers wonder if it's worth investing in. The answer is that, if the only thing they're using it for is public transport, it's not. That's because there are cheaper alternatives, which are...

Tell me more about these unlimited passes...

Rome's transport agency, called ATAC, has its own unlimited transport passes. They can be purchased at any *tabaccaio* or at ticket counters at the metro stations, and they include unlimited access to the metro system, buses and trams.

Before you spring for one, you may want to see first how much you wind up taking public transport: because of how walkable Rome is, and how much you'll want to explore on foot, you may take it less than you'd think. But if you do like the freedom of being able to jump on and off buses, this can be an economical and, more so, convenient way to go than buying a €1.50 ticket each time (especially since you can't buy tickets on the buses).

Here are your options for unlimited passes:

•Roma 24H: As you might expect, this pass covers a full 24 hours on Rome's public transport; it costs €7.

•Roma 48H: 48 hours; €12.50.

•Roma 72H: 72 hours; €18.

•CIS: One week (I guess naming it the Roma 168H didn't roll off the tongue!), but note that unlike the others, this one goes by calendar, not hours – in other words, it cuts off at midnight on the seventh day after you've first validated it. Cost: €24.

Don't forget to "validate"

As you may have heard elsewhere, whether you get your ticket on the bus or in advance at a tobacco shop or metro stop, just having a ticket isn't enough. You also have to validate your ticket (unless you used the ticket, already, to ride the metro – in which case it was stamped by the machine at the turnstile). Usually there are two small, yellow machines on the bus, at the front and back. As soon as you board, feed your ticket through to get it validated, i.e. stamped with the time. Remember that, if it's a single-use ticket, it's good for the next 100 minutes.

You need to validate your ticket to avoid getting a fine. Instead of having the driver check your ticket when you get on the bus, guards are (occasionally) sent onto buses at random stops to check all the passengers for their tickets. Passengers without a validated ticket get fined.

For what it's worth, these checks happen very, very rarely. While living in Rome, I took the bus at least once a day, and was checked only once or twice a year. However, they are completely random – so it's always best to validate!

Now, let's say you got on a bus and thought you had a ticket on you, but you don't. Or you thought you were within your 100 minutes, but you weren't. Or you forgot to validate your ticket. And a guard boards the bus and checks you. What happens next?

Most likely, the guard will tell you your options, which are paying €50 in cash on the spot… or getting a fine sent to you at your home address, to the tune of €100 or more.

The offer of cash-in-pocket seems a little sketchy. But it's not. It's even written on the sign with ticket prices that you should see when you get on the bus (albeit in Italian). My best guess is that they have the two separate fees because they know that, if they send you a fine at your home address, it will most likely 1) not ever arrive or 2) not ever be paid. (That's particularly true in your case, as you'll have returned back to your home country and will never be forced to deal with the fine – certainly not by your home government, but most likely not by Italy, either… I'm not sure they're extraditing for €100 fines these days). By offering you the cash option instead, they know they have at least *some* of the money. It's up to you, of course, to decide how to proceed – but you do have the right to insist that it be sent to you rather than to pay on the spot.

Rome's metro system

In terms of reliability and speed, I tend to think that Rome's metro (or subway) system is remarkably good. I've never waited longer than five minutes for the next train. (I can't say the same for most other cities I've been in, from D.C. to New York). A handy little display tells you how many minutes away the next metro is, like London's Tube.

On the other hand, it can be crowded, especially during rush hour. And in the summer, the air-conditioning doesn't work on all of the cars – meaning it can get stuffy and sweaty. But to travel longer distances in Rome, it's still your best option.

To understand Rome's metro system, you first need to know that, in the center, there are only *two lines*. Just two! (That will change in the not too-distant future as construction on Rome's third line, Line C, crawls toward the center, but even that won't have a huge impact for many tourists, since the most useful stop will be where there already is one – at the Colosseum). The line names are even easier to remember: Line A and Line B. The only point they cross at is Termini (also home to Rome's major train station), so if you have to switch lines, you'll do so there.

Line A includes stops for the Vatican (*Ottaviano* or *Cipro*), Piazza del Popolo (*Flaminio*), Spanish Steps (*Spagna*), and San Giovanni in Laterano (*San Giovanni*).

Line B includes stops at the Colosseum (*Colosseo*), Circus Maximus (*Circo Massimo*), Aventine (*Aventino*), and Testaccio (*Piramide*).

Because, at any metro station except for Termini, there's only *one* metro line, the only choice you have to make is which direction to go in. And it's pretty intuitive. At the entrance to the platform, you'll see a sign listing the stops the metro takes. If the stop you want is bolded, that's the correct direction. If it's grayed out, you're going the wrong way.

Now, here's the problem with Rome's metro: It doesn't cut through most of the *centro storico*. So the metro is great for getting from, say, the Spanish Steps to the Vatican, but not for getting to Piazza Navona, the Pantheon, or myriad other sites in the center.

That's where the buses come in.

Rome's buses and trams

In the historic center, the buses and trams are *fairly* reliable. (Trams are especially trustworthy; the #8 from Largo Argentina to

Trastevere, for example, departs every 5 or 10 minutes on the dot). They also go all over the place, even down those narrow, winding streets that you wouldn't expect smart cars to venture down, never mind city buses. Especially if your feet are feeling tired, they can be a lifesaver.

But that doesn't mean that they're an easy option for those who are new to Rome.

Like the rest of Rome's infrastructure, the bus system here was built for locals. For example: Instead of having maps at each bus stop, showing you the routes, Rome's stops instead have the bus number with its stops listed, below, by name. Obviously, this assumes that you know Rome well enough to know what name refers to which part of the city.

And it's not always self-evident. Piazza Navona, for example, isn't listed on these bus signs as "Piazza Navona" (look for "*Rinascimento*" or "*Zanardelli*", both of which refer to streets next to the piazza, instead). Piazza Venezia can be "*Venezia*", "*Piazza Venezia*" (...so far, so good) or "*Aracoeli*" (shorthand for the church next to it, Santa Maria in Aracoeli). If you get on a bus that stops at "*San Pietro*", you might wind up a little farther from St. Peter's Basilica than you bargained for: That stop refers to the *San Pietro* (or "St. Peter's") *train* station. And don't make the mistake of getting on a bus that stops at "*Cavour*" if you want to go to the Cavour *metro* stop: You'll wind up at a piazza near the Vatican, on the other side of the city!

Confused? I hear you.

But there's a solution. Well, two.

The old-school way, of course, was asking a local. This can be fun (particularly if you want to flex your Italian), but it also has its pitfalls. While foolproof when it comes to major sights, for smaller sights, streets, restaurants, or hotels, it's pretty risky... especially as I've noticed that many Romans don't seem to like to admit when they have no idea. When I first moved to Rome, my faith in asking locals for advice provided me with all kinds of wild goose chases. Of course, the wandering was half the fun. Sometimes, though, I kind of wished someone had just told me "*Non lo so*" rather than sending me in the wrong direction.

These days, of course, few people even think of that as the go-to option. We all have our phones. And while Google Maps was relatively slow to hook up to Rome's public transport network – the reason why, in the last version of this book, I had an entire section on how to use the inelegant-but-functional trip planner on the ATAC website, instead – it now, happily, has. So if you need to get somewhere and you don't know how, do as the Romans (and New Yorkers, and Londoners) do. Pop it in Google Maps and click the public transport option.

A few more words on navigating by bus

If you opt to take the bus, remember that some come far more often than others. And one bus that usually comes every 10 minutes might, when *you* try to get it, take 25 minutes to arrive. Sod's law tends to apply even more in Rome than other cities. Plus, only some of the stops tell you when the next bus is arriving, and even that information can be wrong.

Luckily, if you're going from one major stop to another major stop, there probably will be more than one bus you can take. So when you're waiting, always look at the signs (or look at your Google Maps options) to see if any other bus stopping here is going where you want to go.

Taking a taxi in Rome

If public transportation sounds like too much to handle, you might find yourself relying on taxis to get around.

The bad news: As you might be able to tell from my story about Ciampino, depending on the honesty of your taxi driver, that's not always a foolproof option. The good news: I can help.

In short, I can't tell you how many times I've heard of travelers to Rome getting taken advantage of by their drivers. I've heard of everything from drivers charging fresh-off-the-plane tourists €90 or €100 to get from Fiumicino airport into Rome (the cost should be €48; read the previous section on how to travel from the airports to the center if you haven't already) to pretending that a passenger gave them a different bill than they did and insisting on "the rest".

Worrying about whether you're being taken advantage of isn't pleasant. That, combined with the facts that Rome is a *very* walkable city, public transportation isn't half bad and even Uber is now an option (albeit only in the pricier categories – UberBLACK, UberLUX or UberVAN), means I recommend that, whenever possible, a taxi be your last choice for getting around.

That said? Sometimes, you just have to hop in a cab. And most of the time, you'll be just fine doing so.

But before you do, here are some tips.

Make sure your taxi is official
In Rome, registered taxis are white, have a "TAXI" sign on the roof, and a Rome "SPQR" crest on the doors.

Never accept a ride from a driver who approaches you at the airport or train station
These drivers aren't legal… and they will probably rip you off.

Have cash on you (and if you have small bills, all the better)
I've yet to take at taxi in Rome that accepted credit cards. To avoid an awkward, and expensive, ten minutes with the meter running while the driver goes out of the way to a ATM and then waits for you while you take out your money, have cash already at hand. Try to avoid having only a €100, €50 or even €20 bill: It gives the driver far too much excuse to say he just doesn't have change.

Don't negotiate a flat rate…
Occasionally, when you get in a cab in Rome and say you want to go to a popular tourist site, the driver will offer you a particular fare. Never accept it. The driver knows the city better than you do, and if they're offering you a flat rate they've made up themselves, you can rest assured it's *not* to your advantage. Instead, insist that

the meter be run.

...but know when the city's flat rates help you (and what they are)

The city of Rome has set flat rates to go from the city center to the Ciampino and Fiumicino airports. And these often help you, so make sure you write them down!

As mentioned earlier, the cost for a taxi, *including all luggage and any extra charges,* is €48 from the center of Rome to Fiumicino. It's €30 from the center of Rome (including Trastevere and the Vatican neighborhood) to Ciampino. If you have any doubt about whether the hotel is in the *centro storico,* ask your hotel in advance.

Always give as specific of an address as possible

There are hundreds of hotels, restaurants, and museums in Rome – and many cab drivers just don't know all of them. Not every cab driver has a GPS, either, so unless you want to go on a wild search for directions (with the meter running), provide as specific of an address as possible.

A couple of potential pitfalls: The "Vatican" can mean anywhere around Vatican City, so make sure you say "St. Peter's Basilica" or "Vatican museums". And the "Villa Borghese" means anywhere in the park, so if you want to go to the Borghese *Gallery,* say so. If you want to be incredibly extra prepared, you can write the name of where you want to go down on a card, in Italian (or have your hotel or Airbnb host do it for you), but that's rarely necessary.

Don't panic if the route feels "scenic"

Lots of meandering, one-way roads in Rome mean that, sometimes, a route can feel bizarre – but often still is the fastest way. So if you can't immediately figure out where your driver is taking you, relax. Unless he's simultaneously telling you that he's giving you a "tour of Rome" and "showing you the sights". Then you can put your foot down.

Have an idea of the fares

Just because the meter is running doesn't always mean the driver has set it to the appropriate rate. On Monday through Saturday, from 6am to 10pm, the meter should start at €3; on Sundays, it's €4.50. And after 10pm, on any day, it starts at €6.50. Somewhat quaintly, there's also a 10% discount for "unaccompanied women" taking a taxi between 10am and 6pm.

Extra charges can sometimes be added, but know if they should be or not. The first piece of luggage is free; after that, it's €1 each. Every passenger for more than four passengers is €1. And if you've called a taxi to have it come get you (or if your hotel has), the meter starts from when the cab picks you up, *but* a supplement of €3.50 is added.

When paying, count your euros *slowly*

One trick nefarious drivers like to use: After you've handed them a bill you thought was a €50, they say it was actually a €10, since the color is similar, and insist on "the rest."

Embarrassingly, this recently happened to me; it was late at night, I was tired, and when I went to pay, the driver didn't turn the light on. I handed him what I thought was a €20 – only for him to say it was actually €5. I didn't have any other money on me, so my immediate response was to be flustered and try to figure out where the closest ATM was.

Unfortunately, my lack of thinking continued all the way through my paying him the €10 extra I thought I owed him… and as soon as I entered my house, I realized I actually, definitely *had* given him €20. I felt like an idiot. Don't let it happen to you. Especially if you're unfamiliar with Europe's colorful "Monopoly money", count your bills slowly, deliberately, and in good light (as for any car, there always is a light overhead for the back seats; ask your driver if you need help finding the switch).

Chapter 4
En Route to Rome

Graffiti and Crime

Some big questions usually pop up either before, or shortly after, a visitor has arrived in Rome: How safe is the city? How can I protect myself and avoid being scammed? And (last but not least) why is there so much graffiti here? They aren't pleasant topics, but they're worth getting out of the way. Here's what to know.

How safe is Rome, really?

As in any city, you need to be aware in Rome. It's an urban area. There are lots of people, and not all of them are stand-up characters. Use common sense: Don't walk alone down unlit streets, be aware of your surroundings, don't carry lots of cash on you, and know the country's emergency numbers.

I think it's important, though, also to have a little perspective.

To begin with, a personal impression. In the several years I lived in Rome's *centro storico* as a young, single woman, and today as

I continue to go back, I have never felt physically threatened or otherwise concerned for my safety. That includes times I've walked home late at night, by myself. Of course, I'm always aware of my surroundings, and I use common sense – avoiding dark, empty streets late at night, for example. But I think it still bears mentioning, as I've often heard from other young women planning to travel to Rome alone who are concerned about whether they can explore the city, alone and safely. You might get some *"Ciao bella"* comments, but in general, there are people on Rome's streets at all time of the day and night; keep your wits about you (and avoid potential risks, like going out at night to bars by yourself and accepting random drinks), and you'll be as safe – or safer – than you would in most other big cities.

Which brings me to my next point. As an aside, I know that crime statistics aren't perfect. There are serious issues with crime reporting, not to mention with how to analyze the numbers. Still, I think some solid numbers are more helpful than yet more anecdotal evidence, which is already pretty plentiful on travel forums and elsewhere on the internet. Keep in mind that those anecdotes can be risky, since of course a traveler is much more likely to post about a mugging than to post about *not* having been mugged.

First, let's take the most violent of violent crimes: Murder. According to ISTAT, which collects Italy's crime data per city, there are 0.7 homicides per 100,000 people in Rome as of 2015, the latest statistics available. That makes Rome safer than Venice (1.1 homicides), Milan (1) and Naples (3.9). Historically, that also makes Rome safer than many other European cities – Dublin, Prague, London and Paris among them. Meanwhile, it means all of these cities in Europe are far safer than most U.S. cities. The FBI reports that, for 2015 (the most recent year available), there were 3 homicides per 100,000 people in Seattle, for example, while there were 10.6 in Omaha and 8.6 in Anchorage. The worst city was St. Louis, with 59 homicides. As was reported by *The Economist* in 2016, out of the 50 cities in the world with the highest homicide rates, all are from Latin America and the Caribbean – except for

South Africa and the U.S.

So that's that for murders. But what about other crimes?

The one you're probably already most aware of in Italy, after all, is pickpocketing. And in that sense, you're correct to be alert. While finding rates for petty crime is notoriously difficult, the U.S. Department of State notes that it is the one thing tourists should be alert for in Rome, as any other kind of violent crime is quite rare, and that it has been increasing slightly in the last few years. So you'll definitely want to read on to the next section for tips on how to avoid becoming a victim.

Finally, in one of the less welcome updates I'd like to have to do for this book, many travelers to Europe, these days, aren't as concerned about random manslaughter as they are a terrorist act. This has not, thank God, yet been something Rome has had to deal with. But it is a concern. (Albeit one that Romans have responded to with typical humor: After ISIS made a somewhat enigmatic announcement about the fall of Rome, Romans took to social media to respond with things like, "Don't come over lunch, everything will be closed!" and "Avoid the train, it's always late!"). That's why you'll find security measures stepped up, particularly at some tourist sights. Recently the Colosseum banned backpacks from being taken inside, for example.

There is no way to know what will happen in the future, of course, but as horrific as the acts are which we've seen in places like Paris, Istanbul, Orlando and London, a little perspective remains important. Despite the headlines, anywhere in Europe, you're still more likely to be killed by a fall, a traffic accident or even a lightning strike than by a terrorist act. That isn't meant to be glib; I can't imagine many things more horrific than some of the scenes we've seen recently. But it is meant to point out that, as much as some tragedies have more emotional resonance than others, your actual likelihood of being affected is – and, even today, remains – very low.

It is also worth noting that, sadly, dealing with terrorism isn't new for Europe (or the world, for that matter). In terms of numbers, we aren't even in an especially dangerous moment, as much as it might seem otherwise. Many people in Italy today still remember the 1980 bombings at Bologna's train station that killed 85 people, making it the fourth-worst terrorist attack in Europe, and which was one of a spate of bombings carried out by the Mafia over several decades. Or the numerous bombings by the IRA in Britain. As the BBC has pointed out, while terror attacks in western Europe have become deadlier since the mid-2000s, they affect fewer people than in the past. More than 150 people per year were killed by terrorism in the 1970s and 1980s, compared to about 50 since 1990.

In sum, do you have to be alert and aware of your surroundings in Rome? Yes. But do you also have to be when you're traveling in Paris, or Madrid, or London, or even you're back at home in Dublin or Boston or Omaha? Absolutely. In some cases, even more so.

How to avoid being pickpocketed in Rome

All of that being said, the problem in Rome you'll need to be most aware of is petty crime, specifically pickpocketing. It still is not something you have to be paranoid about. But it does happen – just as it does in Barcelona, or Paris, or Istanbul. And there's no quicker way to ruin a vacation than to reach into your pocket and discover that your wallet's been lifted.

Here's the thing to remember: Most pickpockets are *very* talented. Once they've picked you as their target, you may need to kiss that wallet goodbye. One part of the key is to not get picked as their target to begin with.

Forget trying "not to look like a tourist"

As mentioned earlier, unless you're a gifted style chameleon and already have a wardrobe of Italy-bought items, you won't look like an Italian. And even if you *are* wearing something lifted from an Italian fashion blog, something else will give you away – your hand gestures, your haircut, even your smile. That's *before* you open your mouth and start speaking English, or Italian with a foreign accent.

So while it feels nice to blend in as much as possible, know that you probably won't be able to "pass". Not to mention that people who regularly encounter tourists – from waiters to tour guides to, yes, pickpockets – will be especially attuned to being able to tell if you're a tourist or not. It's not a bad thing. It's just a fact.

But *do* try not look like a clueless tourist...

Some items of clothing will mark you as not just a tourist, but one who hasn't traveled much. And *that* can make you a particular target. Again, I mean the classics here, like the big white sneakers, fanny packs (or "bum bags"), sweatsuits and sweatpants, and T-shirts printed with "I LOVE ROME".

Fairly or not, these items aren't just interpreted as "I'm a tourist"; they're interpreted as "I'm a tourist, and I'm on my first trip abroad *ever*, and that's why I'll be too busy staring at the Colosseum or looking through my postcards to notice you going through my pockets!". In other words, an invitation.

Or to act like one

Put simply, you should always be aware of what's going on around you, especially if you're in a very crowded area or a very quiet, dark one. For example, here are some things *not* to do:

•when getting that perfect photo, don't focus on your camera (or phone) so much that you wouldn't notice someone coming up behind you

•at an outdoor restaurant or café, don't leave your purse dangling off the back of your chair, or sitting on the ground next to you

•at a café or bar, don't leave your phone or wallet on the countertop next to you while you have a coffee (or glass of wine)

•don't get so engrossed in a conversation on the bus (or in your phone) that neither of you notice the person taking the opportunity to lift a wallet out of your purse

I've seen all four of these situations happen. Every time, they could have been avoided.

Know the classic tricks

If you're in a crowd and you're suddenly, inexplicably shoved, that's a red flag. As you catch your balance, your hands go up (away from your purse or pockets), you stop paying attention for a split second... and it's the perfect moment to lift your wallet.

Another telltale sign is when you're on a metro or bus that's packed to the gills and someone forces their way on – despite there being clearly no room at all. Of course, lots of people try to shove on, particularly around rush hour. But if you see someone who seems even more determined than most, and especially if you then see them continue to work their way through the bus, despite the crowd, that's a sign of something fishy.

Another classic pickpocketing trick: Boarding the metro right before the doors close, grabbing a wallet (perhaps with the shove-and-surprise move), and then exiting just as the doors are closing.

Also be aware when you see a group of several people begging on a street or along a crowd. There will be a child or two, or a cardboard sign, or sometimes both. Stop to read the sign, and a child gets you from your back pocket. Turn to the child, and someone's pickpocketing you while using the sign as cover. (This happens less frequently than it used to – I haven't seen it in a few years in Rome – but still good to be on the lookout for).

Finally, don't make the mistake of assuming that the person who looks a bit suspicious is working alone. The one time, after moving to Rome, I found my own purse unzipped (more on that at the end of this section), I can only assume it's because the person I thought looked suspicious was working with someone else who I didn't suspect. So if something seems "off", of any reason, don't just turn away from the person you don't trust; add some extra protection, like moving your bag to the front of your body, making sure it's securely closed and has your arm over it, as well.

Clearly, you can't know every trick in the book. Fortunately, since it *isn't* likely you'll encounter these scenarios on one or two trips to Rome, you don't have to.

But if something strikes you as "off," like someone jamming their way into a bus or knocking into you, trust that instinct, try to maneuver away from that person and make sure anything valuable is well out of reach.

Choose a purse or money belt that makes a pickpocket's life hard

As I said in my section on packing, I don't think it's necessary to have a money belt in Rome. It always strikes me as a little paranoid, as well as inconvenient – every time you buy a gelato or a museum ticket, you have to reach down under your shirt or pants and take out cash? And if you're in a high-risk situation, what's to stop someone from pickpocketing you at *that* moment?

Still, we're talking about the best ways to deter pickpockets here. And wearing a money belt can be one of them, as long as it's the right kind of money belt. One that goes over your clothes is useless. It's particularly useless if it's back-facing (like a fanny pack).

In general, though, I tend to think a purse or wallet is fine. Wallets should always be carried in a front pocket, not a back pocket. In certain (crowded) situations, be sure to keep your hand on the pocket which has the wallet in it.

Purses should have a zip top; no outside pockets (at least that you put anything important in); a separate, zipped compartment inside for your wallet, if possible; and should still be carried at the front of your body, with your arm over the top, when in a potentially "high-risk" situation (see below).

Don't carry ridiculous amounts of cash

Although I think most of you already will know this, it bears repeating, since I once read a money belt review online saying the traveler safely carried around €800 in cash on their trip. It speaks highly of the money belt... because that's an absurd thing to do!

If this is something you're considering, I get it: You want to minimize the amount of ATM fees by taking out a lot of money at once. And you're worried you won't find an ATM when you *do* need cash. But you're in a city. There are lots of ATMs everywhere. And I'd rather spend $5 or even $10 extra per transaction to not have to worry that, if something happened, I'd be out $1,000.

At the very least, don't carry that much on you because, when you're going into your money belt to take a bill out of that thick wad of cash, people (and potential pickpockets) will see that you're Mr. (or Ms.) Moneybags.

Perhaps the *most important* tip: Remember that context is key

You could make all of these mistakes while sitting on a bench in quiet Piazza Farnese, or looking at a mosaic in the Palazzo Massimo, or while sightseeing on the Palatine Hill, and—most likely—you'd still leave with your belongings intact. That's because, although you should always be aware of your surroundings, these types of situations—where you're in an uncrowded area, especially one where you have to pay to be there—are ones where you can generally let your guard down.

When you have to be careful is when you're 1) in the tourist crowds and 2) it's easy to access you (and your pockets) and leave, all without 3) much monetary investment on the pickpocket's part.

So while you can relax a bit in the Sistine Chapel (seriously, what pickpocket wants to pay €15 *and*, if he's caught, be stuck in an enclosed space?), *do* be especially aware at the Termini train station, Trevi Fountain, Spanish Steps, Porta Portese market, and Colosseum. Also be highly cautious on crowded buses and subway trains.

Finally: Relax!

Is it more likely you'd be pickpocketed in Rome than in a small town somewhere else (including in Italy, for that matter)? Yes. Is it still really unlikely anything bad will happen to you? Yes.

My wallet was lifted from my purse once in Rome. It was a decade ago, on a trip when I was visiting as a tourist before moving to the city a couple of years later. I'd made every mistake in the book: I had a big purse with my wallet lying right on top of everything else, everything was unzipped and open, and my purse was pushed around toward the back of my body, not the front. I also wasn't paying any attention, at all.

When I moved to Rome and became a little more street-savvy, this never happened to me again, despite taking public transportation at least once or twice a day and often being in crowds. I did, however, see it happen to others several times. Once, a thief stole a woman's handbag that she had left dangling off the back of her seat, at a cafe in a mall, and ran off. Another time, I came upon a couple of tourists who just had been mugged; they had been alone in the Colle Oppio park, overlooking the Colosseum, as the sun set and had fancy, expensive cameras that they had set on tripods. Especially because they were focused on their shot, they were, unfortunately, prime targets for a mugging.

But these are incidents that I saw over years of not only living in the city, but spending a great deal of time out and about in it. Unlike most, I didn't take the metro to work, stay in an office all day and come home. Rather, I usually spent hours each day at Rome's sights and on its streets.

Most importantly, all of these incidents have one thing in common. They could have been avoided. So be aware, be savvy, but also relax. The only thing worse than being pickpocketed is spending your trip paranoid about being pickpocketed... and it's highly unlikely you'll be a victim yourself.

The most popular scams in Rome

While we're on the subject of less pleasant things, petty crime isn't the only thing to keep your eye out for in Rome. Like pickpocketing, being scammed isn't something you should expect to experience. But it is something to know about in advance so that if you're in the wrong situation, at the wrong time, you at least have the right response.

A few years ago, there were a number of street scams that were very concrete and very common – like the rose-as-a-gift gambit. Thankfully, it seems Rome has cleaned up a bit, and you run into these far less often. What you do still see, though, are scams that are in a slightly grayer area – more along the lines of manipulating tourists rather than outright cheating them. In the interest of making sure you're as prepared as possible, I've included all of the above below.

Again, it's unlikely you'll run into many of these in your short time in the city. But it's good to recognize them if (or when) you see them.

Being told you "need" a tour

If you've shown up to the Vatican museums, St. Peter's Basilica or Colosseum and you're approached by someone who tells you that you "need" a tour in order to skip the line – or that you're wrong and your ticket won't actually take you into the Sistine Chapel or something else you thought it would – be wary. Some of these "gatherers" do, in fact, work for companies that do have skip-the-line privileges, so if you haven't already figured out a way to skip the line (hopefully ahead of your trip, but if not, by using one of the tips I'll share later), they may save you time. The problem is, though, the industry of off-the-street tours is the wild west (complete with criminal involvement and lots of cash changing hands) – and you don't know for sure if you've gotten one of the relatively "good" companies until you've already committed.

It's also worth noting that, usually, even companies that do let you skip the line legitimately will still make you wait until they've "gathered" a group together that's large enough to enter with. Other times, companies don't have legitimate privileges, so they'll force you into the line – which is not only unfair and awkward, but not exactly worth whatever premium you're paying (you could have just muscled in yourself!). And sometimes, as when they tell you your officially purchased Vatican museum ticket doesn't include the Sistine Chapel, they're outright lying. The problem, of course, is that when a friendly, English-speaking expat or Italian approaches you with the seemingly-helpful offer of skipping the line, you won't have any idea which of the above categories they fall into. So while I'm not saying every tour gathered from the street is a scam, the industry itself isn't exactly honest. I can't stress it enough: book in advance to avoid being in this situation at all, and do consider taking a tour – but one from a legitimate company that you research ahead of time.

Usually seen: At the Vatican and Colosseum

Most likely victims: Any tourists, but particularly those who look surprised to see a line outside the site.

How common is it? So common, it's unlikely you won't be approached on your way to the Vatican museums or Colosseum.

If it happens to you? Say you already have your ticket (or tour) and you're sure that it allows you to see everything you'd like, but thanks anyway.

The many types of taxi scams

Many Rome taxi drivers are honest. Some are not. As you may remember from the previous section on taking taxis in Rome, those who are not tend to repeat some of the same ploys. One popular one is not using the meter, either by saying it's broken, "forgetting" to turn it on, or giving you a flat fee up front, usually something absurd like €20 to get from the Colosseum to the Vatican. None of those things, of course, are legal. Another is refusing to accept the city-set flat rates from Rome's airports to the historic center, or claiming that's just the fare to the city walls themselves. (If you missed it before, more on this scam here).

Another popular scam is to run the meter, but adjust it to make the fare higher. For example, the driver can put the meter on *Zona* (or *Tariffa*) 2; that should only apply for rides outside Rome's beltway, and is a lot more expensive than *Zona 1*, the proper zone if you're anywhere within the historic center. Or the driver might set it to the night rate, which starts at €6.50 rather than €30, earlier than its 10pm starting time. Or he might just take a circuitous route to get someplace (this is the toughest for tourists to tell, since many of Rome's streets are one-way and getting around actually is tricky).

Usually seen: Anywhere in the center or at the airports, but especially with taxis whose drivers try to "hawk" you and at spots with lots of tourists, like the Termini station or the Colosseum.

Most likely victims: Any tourists.

How common is it? You won't run into it every time you take a taxi (like you'll run into tour gatherers every time you go to the Vatican), but it's still rather common. Even I've been scammed more than once.

If it happens to you? In this case, the best is prevention. Avoid taking taxis unless you have to, have a rough idea of what the fare should be, and make sure you get into the car with small bills on you. When you get in, look to see if the meter is on; if it's not, ask (or insist) that it be turned on, or get out of the car. Same for the set rates from the airports: As you're getting into the car, say "I'm going to X place. That's €48/€30, right?" to head off any problems at the pass. Again, if the driver resists at all, just get out of the car.

If you're already en route or at your destination and having problems, don't despair. Be firm, argue – and if all else fails, hand the correct amount of cash over and no more (that's where the small bills come in handy). Don't hesitate to threaten to get the police involved before you hand over cash, either. The taxi drivers don't want this, so most likely they'll back down or let you out far before it escalates to that point.

The open-water scam

Some of the food vans as well as cafés in more touristic areas deliberately don't have signs up, or clearly visible, with prices for everything – especially things that visitors tend to grab and immediately swill, like bottles of water. Because many people assume that a bottle of water won't be that expensive, they're caught unaware when they go to pay, and many, out of embarrassment or because they've just waited in line, will pay the €3, €5 or even €10 that's asked. (Keep in mind that if you went to any grocery store nearby instead, you'd pay €0.80 for the same bottle of water). Worse still, though, is if you've already unscrewed the cap and started to drink: In that case, you're just about stuck.

Usually seen: At various food vans and cafés in the historic center, including around the Colosseum and Vatican and at cafés near the Spanish Steps and Piazza del Popolo.

Most likely victims: Any tourists.

How common is it? Fairly common if you get something to eat or drink at one of the touristic food vans around the Vatican or Colosseum. (But, really, why would you do that?) A bit less common at cafés – but still something to be aware of, since some are notorious for doing this.

If it happens to you? Head this one off early: If you grab an item, if you can't see a price, ask. Otherwise, even if you're already at the cashier, don't be afraid (or embarrassed) to change your mind. If you have already opened your purchase, it's a little more difficult – though, especially if the amount being asked for is egregious, you still can refuse. If it escalates, put down whatever you've gone to purchase and simply walk away, or insist on calling the police.

The *prego,* take a seat trick

Again, this one's a gray area and certainly not illegal, but I'm including it because it catches many visitors unaware. Cafés in Rome (and throughout Italy) often have two different prices: One for taking your coffee, snack or whatever else at the counter (called the bar in Italy); the other for sitting at a table. The reason is that the table often comes with "service" – literally just someone bringing you your drink, and then your bill. The food and drink can be three times as expensive to have that way, which is okay if you realize that, but less so if you don't. To make matters worse, some hosts will tell tourists to take a seat as they pass, or – if they've gone in to order at the bar – will tell them no, don't worry about it, go sit outside, I'll bring you your food. Later, when the bill arrives, the same visitors wonder how on earth Italians can afford to drink so much coffee out!

Usually seen: At cafés in the historic center.

Most likely victims: Any tourists.

How common is it? Almost every café in Rome's historic center has this two-price scenario, so unless you know the situation, it could happen anywhere.

If it happens to you? Again, prevention is best. Take your coffee standing up (as locals tend to do) if you can. Otherwise, there should be a price list on the wall around the bar that you can scan to see what the difference will be if you sit at a table (if there isn't a list, be wary). And always feel free to tell the host "No, *grazie*, we'll take coffee at the bar."

The "service is not included" ploy

Again, not technically a scam – but something that really makes me angry when I see it. Italians don't have a tipping culture; most locals will round up on a bill by leaving a few coins on the table, but that still means paying far less than some other nationalities, particularly Americans, tend to do (think leaving €50 for a €47 bill). While I know it makes some travelers uncomfortable, I strongly believe that visitors to Italy should do the same. (More on why, and on tipping in Italy, later). But that doesn't mean that servers don't love large cash tips – or that they don't know Americans are used to giving them. To "help" that happen, at some restaurants, the waiter will leave the bill with a pointed comment: "The tip is not included." A local's response? Of course it's not – *servizio* rarely is – and how manipulative of the server to point that out! But an (American) tourist often will take the hint at that, leaving behind a hefty 20% extra. That's an even bigger boon to the server when a 10% or 12% *servizio* was, in fact, already on the bill – as it is at some tourist spots.

Usually seen: At cafés in the historic center.

Most likely victims: Any tourists.

How common is it? You're unlikely to see it at most local, authentic spots, but diner beware if you're at the restaurants (particularly those with all of the outdoor seating and tourist menus) in areas such as around the Pantheon or Piazza Navona.

If it happens to you? They're trying to manipulate you because you're a tourist, which means there's only one response: Ignore the suggestion and leave no tip at all.

The just-helping-you-with-your-ticket trick

You're fumbling at a ticket machine for the metro or train, trying to figure out what to press on the screen. Like magic, someone appears to help you. Once your ticket is printed, they then ask you for a few coins as a tip. Once you realize that you could have figured it out without them, it might just have taken ten seconds longer… you feel slightly foolish.

Usually seen: At the Termini train station and at metro stations with lots of tourists, like Colosseo.

How common is it? Far less common than it used to be, thanks to an increased security presence at Rome's stations, but still something to be aware of.

Most likely victims: Tourists, or anyone else who doesn't look like they know what they're doing.

If it happens to you? Shake your head and say "no" when that ever-so-helpful someone appears. Don't be afraid to be polite, but very firm.

The "rose-as-a-gift" gambit

You're female, traveling with a male companion. A stranger comes up to you and tells you that you're so beautiful, he just has to give you a red rose. You take it, thrilled. You and your husband/boyfriend/brother start to walk away. After precisely five beats, the kind stranger suddenly reappears. "Please, two euros for the rose," he says to your male companion. "Okay, a euro."

The poor guy is forced either to pay for the "free" rose, or to make you give it back, making himself look like a jerk. Don't want to put your husband/friend in that situation? Don't accept the rose.

Usually seen: At the Spanish Steps, Pantheon or Trevi Fountain, or at restaurants in touristy areas in the center.

How common is it? This used to be impossible to avoid, particularly in the Spanish Steps area, especially in the evening. Today, it's pretty rare to see, but worth knowing about (I've see it in other cities, too).

Most likely victims: Tourists in couples.

If it happens to you? Unless you want the rose (and maybe you do! It'll make their day if that's the case!) hand it back politely, but firmly, and don't feel guilty. These guys do this hundreds of times a day.

ATM fraud

You use an ATM to withdraw money – usually, the best way to avoid extra fees. When you get home and check your bank statement, you realize someone else has been withdrawing money, as well.

This is getting more common as more and more criminals are figuring out ways to install ATM skimming devices onto the machines, which can capture your account information by using a card reader and a tiny video camera to capture your PIN.

Usually seen: Unpredictable.

How common is it? It's never happened to me, but I've heard of funky things happening at ATMs more than once.

Most likely victims: Anyone using an ATM.

If it happens to you: There's not much you can do, although of course once you file the fraud with your bank, you should get the money returned.

The best way to avoid this, though, is to always cover the keypad with your hands when you type in your PIN and, when possible, to use the ATMs that are *inside* reputable banks. If it looks like you need to slide a card through a scanner to get into the vestibule, don't worry – whatever your bank card is will work. Also be wary of any gaps or tampered appearance in the machine, and avoid card readers that aren't flush with the machine's face.

Any distraction technique

These run the gamut. Maybe you're at a busy metro stop and someone collides into you. Maybe you're out at a club and a guy dances up close to you... *really* close. Maybe a little girl tugs on your pant leg and asks you for help. Either way, by the time you've reacted, your wallet is gone.

Usually seen: Everywhere – including, it should be noted, in cities worldwide.

How common is it? As far as pickpocketing strategies go, this one's extremely common.

Most likely victims: Anyone who looks capable of being surprised. In other words, anyone.

If it happens to you: By the time it happens, it's too late. Even if you can chase down the accomplice, your stuff is long-gone. The only way to avoid it is to be aware – and if something feels fishy, like someone colliding into you, it probably is. In that moment, if you can, try to do the opposite of your usual instinct – so if someone rams into you, don't throw your hands in the air, leaving your pocket unprotected; if a child tries to get your attention, put your attention on your valuables instead.

Why is there so much graffiti in Rome?

There's something else you may be curious about in Rome: Graffiti. There is more graffiti in Rome than there tends to be in American or northern European cities. And, as in cities worldwide, there's more graffiti the farther you get from the upscale, expensive city center (and the police). (That being said, if you head to London's Brick Lane neighborhood, or other southern European cities like Athens, you'd see just as much; in some areas, it's even reached an art form – as it has in parts of Rome, too).

But don't mistake graffiti for being the mark of a bad neighborhood. In Rome, it's not. My old neighborhood, Celio, a stone's throw from the Colosseum, is considered pretty upmarket – and there's still graffiti on some of the *palazzi* here.

I'm definitely not saying graffiti is good. But I think a few things are worth noting.

First, as long as people in general, and Romans in particular, have been around, we've had the urge to make our mark. That's as true of cave paintings thousands of years ago as it is of "Alice + Tom 4ever" today.

Second, graffiti isn't always a bad thing. Without ancient graffiti, we wouldn't have the world's oldest example of written Latin, carved into the *lapis niger* in the Forum in 575 B.C. We wouldn't have nearly as much idea of how literate most ancient Romans were, or of how they actually pronounced their language (both of which we can tell from graffiti's misspellings and grammatical errors).

Graffiti also gives us insights – often both humorous and

humanizing – into past cultures. Actual graffiti in Pompeii, for example, includes such winning lines as "Weep, you girls. My penis has given you up. Now it penetrates men's behinds. Goodbye, wondrous femininity!" (bar/brothel of Innulus and Papilio); "Satura was here on September 3rd (atrium of the House of Pinarius); "Atimetus got me pregnant" (House of the Vibii); "Celadus the Thracier makes the girls moan!" (gladiators' barracks); and "If anyone does not believe in Venus, they should gaze at my girlfriend" (atrium of the house of Pinarius) (and... awww!).

And everyone, not just the riffraff of society, has felt the urge to make their mark on buildings and monuments... even those who, it would seem, were making more important marks in other ways. Michelangelo and Raphael both scratched their names into the ruins of Nero's Domus Aurea; American settlers heading west carved inscriptions onto Signature Rock on the Oregon Trail, now a national landmark. Even Lord Byron couldn't resist, scratching his name onto the Temple of Poseidon in Attica, Greece.

I'm not condoning any of this, by the way. I tend to think that the idiotic tourists who recently scratched their names in the Colosseum should be banned from Rome for life. And I agree that most of the graffiti on Rome's buildings (though not all – some of the murals in Ostiense are pretty spectacular) is an irresponsible eyesore. Cleaning it up, meanwhile, is frustrating and expensive: Repainting a four-story palazzo can set you back €40,000.

And so Rome has launched a campaign against the practice. A couple of years ago, the city's mayor raised the fine for graffiti from a minimum €25 to €300 and mandated that anyone caught doing it will be forced to clean the graffiti up. Meanwhile, expats and Italians have started to fight the city's graffiti in volunteer squads, armed with paintbrushes and cleaning solution.

But not everyone's thrilled about these attempts. Critics point to how long graffiti has been around and how impossible it is to prevent, saying that preventing Romans from spray-painting their walls is like forbidding them from ever using slang. For some practitioners, meanwhile, graffiti is an art; for others, it's part of a heated competition to claim physical space in a city where actually buying property is out of most Romans' means.

And in a city where jobs are scarce and creative jobs scarcer, where architectural or artistic innovation rare (the **MAXXI** museum aside), where the old palaces and ancient ruins can make the city feel more like a living museum than an evolving, organic metropolis, where the police aren't particularly notable for being energetic enforcers of the law... that all seems like the kind of place where it's little surprise that a teenager might grab a can of spray-paint and go "tagging" on a hot, lazy summer night.

Nor is it surprising that most Romans, as much as many support a "graffiti offensive," both seem to understand the urge to make one's mark in spray-paint – and refuse to let it bother them.

So: By all means, feel free to think the graffiti makes the city uglier. But if you want to see Rome like a Roman... then you might have to learn to ignore it.

Chapter 5
When in Rome

Sightseeing

You've probably come to Rome mainly to sightsee. So maybe you've already bought the guidebooks. And looked on Tripadvisor. And spoken to friends who have traveled here.

Those are all good things to do. And in no way is this section meant to replace that research. Here's what it does cover:

•some helpful ways to organize your sightseeing

•a few of my favorite sights, including underground sites, places for art lovers and areas where you can sightsee outdoors

•how to schedule your sightseeing in Rome

•last-minute tricks to skip the line and you didn't book a ticket in advance

•where to find the bare necessities: water and the toilet

•some tips for how to sightsee in a way that helps Rome

How do I organize my sightseeing in

Rome?

As you've probably noticed if you've picked up a guidebook, there are dozens, if not hundreds, of sights to see in Rome.

We've already talked about the importance of going into it with some perspective: No, you won't be able to see everything in the city; yes, you're lucky to be able to experience any of it all; and most of all, with the right planning (and attitude), you'll have the experience of your life.

But even with that in mind, how do you wrap your mind around what to see, and how? I get asked this all the time. In fact, in my travel consulting chats, how to choose what to see, and plan when to see it, is probably the number-one question I receive.

The short answer: Think of it in terms of "buckets".

Rome is a compact city. It's also a very walkable one, particularly in the central area which you're likely to find yourself in the most. Even so, it's best to start thinking of in terms of different areas, each with a bucket list of sights and activities. Many guidebooks try to divide their chapters up similarly, of course, but – for the most part – I've noticed that they do it in a way that seems to confuse people more than anything else.

Here are some "buckets" I've used, instead, that people seem to find more helpful. For each, I've included the main sights, how much time to give yourself for those, what you could add if you have more time, tips and tricks to keep in mind and other "buckets" that – thanks to geographic proximity – can be added on if you want to do two (or more) in a day. Because I know most people want to plan their snacks and meals around where they'll be sightseeing anyway, I've also included some of the best restaurants, cafés, gelato shops and bars in each section. You will find more information about my favorites of these in my round-up of favorite food spots later, but I'm including them here as an organizational tool.

This list is not meant to be exhaustive – there are far more neighborhoods in Rome, and far more sights, than are included here. However, I've tried to cover the ones that tend to be of most interest to visitors; if you want to explore further, there's a list of other suggestions (but with only brief descriptions) at bottom.

Primary buckets

If you're short on time (three days or less), it's best to focus on three primary buckets: The heart of the *centro storico* (backdrop to all your Roman Holiday fantasies), ancient Rome (centered on the Colosseum and Forum) and the Vatican (including St. Peter's Basilica and the Sistine Chapel). If you're in Rome for longer, these three chunks still provide a good base for building your trip.

The heart of the *centro storico*

This isn't an official *rione* (neighborhood) – but it's the easiest way to describe the part of the center where most tourists, inevitably, end up. If you look at a map, you'll find that there's a single, straight street (one of the few in Rome!), Via del Corso, that runs from Piazza Venezia (in the south) to Piazza del Popolo (in the north). (It's straight because it was the ancient Roman road that ran out of the city, and was later renamed Via del Corso after the *corse*, or horse races, that took place during Carnevale in later years. But I digress). For our purposes, think of Via del Corso as the "spine" of this area. Then track your eyes around it. You'll notice, in an almost absurdly convenient circle, the recently-restored Spanish Steps and (also recently restored) Trevi Fountain to its east, and the Pantheon and Piazza Navona (to its west) – all anchored by the larger-than-life (many would say grotesque) Victor Emanuel monument at Piazza Venezia to the south.

As you can imagine, this loop alone is a lovely walk and a nice introduction to the city.

What should I keep in mind? First, all of these main sights are outdoors – so if you're coming in the heat of summer, consider doing this walk in the evening. Keep in mind that you'll want to time it so that you can still enter the Pantheon (as of this writing, it closes at 7:15pm in the summer, as early as 4:30pm in the winter). Second, this is the most touristy of all of the areas, so this isn't one where you want to randomly pick a restaurant for lunch or dinner. (Some of my favorites are listed for the area in the next chapter). It's also not one where you want to forget where you put your wallet, especially around the Trevi Fountain and Spanish Steps. Finally, make sure you're up on the various scams that tend to affect Rome's visitors the most.

How much time do I need? Give yourself at least two or three hours to cover only those essential sights.

If I have more time, what else can I add? Here are just a few other sights I'd recommend adding, if you have time, starting at Piazza Venezia and heading north: Palazzo Valentini (more on that next)Basilica di Santa Maria Sopra Minerva (near the Pantheon; stunning Gothic church with a Michelangelo sculpture and beautiful frescoes by Renaissance master Filippino Lippi), Palazzo Altemps (near Piazza Navona; an extremely underrated, little-visited museum of ancient sculpture set in a Renaissance palace), Stadio di Domiziano (near Piazza Navona; also in the next section), Chiostro del Bramante (beautiful cloister designed by Bramante, which often has special exhibitions on); Chiesa di San Luigi dei Francese (near Piazza Navona; home to fantastic Caravaggio paintings), Chiesa di Santa Maria del Popolo (near Piazza del Popolo; also home to fantastic Caravaggio paintings) and the Pincian hill and Villa Borghese (reached via steps at Piazza del Popolo; beautiful park and overlook of Rome).

Where should I eat? For meals in this area, I'd recommend Armando al Pantheon (Pantheon), La Matricianella (north of Parliament), La Campana (Piazza Navona), Da Francesco (Piazza Navona), Pastificio (Spanish Steps – lunch only) and Il Margutta (Piazza del Popolo – vegetarian). For coffee, Sant'Eustachio il Caffè (Pantheon), Tazza d'Oro (Pantheon) and (for the atmosphere) the café at Chiostro del Bramante. For gelato, Vice (near Largo di Torre Argentina).

Other buckets you could add on from here: Ancient Rome; the Jewish Ghetto. If you're going to the Villa Borghese and up for a pretty, 20-minute stroll, you could easily tack on the Borghese Gallery here, as well. Just remember to book in advance.

Ancient Rome

Guidebooks often refer to the area around the Colosseum, Forum and Palatine as "ancient Rome". That can be misleading, as there are bits of ancient Rome strewn throughout the city. But it's an easy shorthand for the fact that these are the ancient ruins where 95% of visitors spend the most time. The bad news is that all three of these sights require a ticket to enter; the good news is that they're all on one single, combined ticket, which makes them easy to put in one "bucket". (If you took me up on my advice about booking the Colosseum in advance, then you already have that ticket in hand).

What should I keep in mind? There is very little in the way of shelter in the Roman Forum, Palatine or even Colosseum – so on a sunny summer day, pace yourself, wear sunscreen and bring water. This is also a place where you're likely to get stopped and asked if you want to take a tour, so if you haven't already, go back to the earlier sections about why you shouldn't take a tour on the street (and tours to consider instead). Finally, although it looks like there is little in this area in the way of sustenance, don't despair: Just head north over the Via dei Fori Imperiali into Monti, one of Rome's best-loved little neighborhoods, for an array of good, authentic spots.

How much time do I need? To cover just the Forum and Colosseum, give yourself at least an hour and a half; if you're heading up Palatine Hill, two hours, minimum. Three hours, or a half-day, to see all three parts will allow you to breathe a bit easier.

Other sights you could add: If you have more time, there are some other sights you could add on top of seeing the Forum, Colosseum and Palatine, including: Palazzo Valentini (on the Piazza Venezia, or western, side of the Via dei Fori Imperiali; no mistake that it's both here and above – it could go in either bucket), the Imperial Forums (across Via dei Fori Imperiali from the Roman Forum; don't miss Trajan's Column), Museo dei Fori Imperiali (across Via dei Fori Imperiali from the Roman Forum; museum dedicated to the Imperial Forums and Trajan's Market), Basilica di San Pietro in

Vincoli (just north of Via dei Fori Imperiali in the neighborhood of Monti; home to the final tomb of Pope Julius II and, accordingly, to Michelangelo's *Moses*), the Domus Aurea (the Golden House of Emperor Nero, recently opened to the public on a limit, pre-booked basis only; re-read the earlier section on "Sights to book in advance" for how to get tickets); the Basilica of San Clemente (located up the street from the Colosseum; a 12th-century basilica ... built on top of a 4th-century basilica ... built on top of ancient Roman ruins – though beware, at the end of 2015 the price doubled to a steep €10 per person to enter, more than almost any other single site in Rome!).

Where should I eat? For meals, L'Asino d'Oro (center of Monti – good lunch deal), Monti Bio (center of Monti), Zia Rosetta (center of Monti – on weekdays lunch only), Alle Carrette (south part of Monti, near the Forum), La Barrique (northwest side of Monti, near Via Nazionale), Ai Tre Scalini (center of Monti), Aromaticus (center of Monti), Li Rioni (on the other side of Colle Oppio, closer to the Colosseum and the Basilica of San Clemente, on the border of Celio and Monti – hence the name, "the neighborhoods") and Il Tajut (also on the Celio/Monti border). For wine and aperitivo, Ai Tre Scalini (center of Monti), Fafiuche' (center of Monti), Al Vino al Vino (center of Monti), DivinOstilia (on the other side of Colle Oppio, closer to the Colosseum and the Basilica of San Clemente) and Il Pentagrappolo (also closer to Colosseum). For coffee, Antico Caffé del Brasile (center of Monti). For baked goods, Panificio Monti and Antico Forno ai Serpenti (both center of Monti). For gelato, Fatamorgana (can you guess? Monti).

Other buckets you could add on from here: The Jewish Ghetto; Aventine; Celio; around Termini.

The Vatican
Because it looks a little bit farther away on a map – it's over the Tiber from the heart of Rome's center – many people plan to spend a whole day on this "bucket", which usually includes the Vatican museums (the Sistine Chapel is inside the complex), St.

Peter's Basilica, and maybe Castel Sant'Angelo. In reality, though, the area is not particularly difficult to get to (if you take the metro from the Spanish Steps, it's about 15 minutes to the Ottaviano stop), and not everyone will want to spend a whole day there. While the surrounding area, which is called the *rione* of Prati, is graceful, continental-European feeling and a popular area for hotels and B&Bs, it's also an area that is a little less chock-full of "must-see" (or "should-see") sights than the rest of the historic center.

What should I keep in mind? If you're heading to the Vatican, you should make sure you have arranged a way to skip the line (check out the "Sights to book in advance" section if you haven't already). As with the area around the Colosseum, you'll want to avoid the on-the-street tour offers. It's also worth keeping in mind that, in summer, sightseeing here is hot: The line to see St. Peter's Basilica is exposed in the sunshine, and the Vatican museums are crowded and without air conditioning, so can be quite sweaty. At the same time, you will need to be dressed relatively modestly to enter St. Peter's and the Sistine Chapel – so bring a scarf to cover bare shoulders, and go with a knee-length skirt (or trousers) rather than anything too short. Finally, again, the touristy nature of the area means that good-value places to eat can be hard to find.

How much time do I need? For the Vatican museums and St. Peter's Basilica alone (assuming you've booked tickets in advance and won't have to stand in lines), at least 2.5 hours. If you plan to walk over to Castel Sant'Angelo, at least four.

Other sights you could add: Aside from a few really esoteric spots, really just Castel Sant'Angelo.

Where should I eat? For meals, Fa-Bio (near Vatican museums entrance – lunch only), Pizzarium (Vatican museums entrance – lunch only), Passaguai (Vatican museum entrance and St. Peter's) and Nuvolari (near St. Peter's). For coffee, Sciascia Caffè (equidistant to Vatican museums, St. Peter's and Castel Sant'Angelo). For wine, Il Sorpasso (Vatican). For gelato, Gelateria dei Gracchi (equidistant to Vatican museums, St. Peter's and Castel Sant'Angelo).

Other buckets you could add on from here: The heart of the *centro storico;* Trastevere.

Secondary buckets

This isn't an exhaustive list of other possible "buckets" (Rome has so much to do and see!). But it does include some of my favorites, all of which can be tacked on to either one of the primary buckets, or can be strung together. Again, for each, I'll include the main sights, how much time to give yourself for those, what you could add if you have more time, tips and tricks to keep in mind and, finally, other "buckets" that – thanks to geographic proximity – can be added on if you want to do two (or more) in a day.

Jewish Ghetto

Forget the modern connotations of the word "ghetto": This is one of the loveliest, most atmospheric areas of Rome. While it is home to the oldest Jewish community in Europe (it dates back to the 2nd century B.C.) and, as you might expect, to a striking synagogue, kosher bakeries and Jewish-Roman trattorias, it shouldn't be considered an area only for visitors interested in Jewish history; it's also full of ancient ruins, pretty piazzas and some very good restaurants. Compact and very pedestrian-friendly, it's one of my favorite places for a stroll.

What should I keep in mind? This area doesn't require a great deal of advance planning, except for one thing: As it is a Jewish area, most shops and restaurants are closed on Friday evening and through Saturday. (This makes it a good place to visit on Mondays as well, of course, as on Christian holidays, when many restaurants elsewhere in Rome can be closed). I'd also caution you to avoid almost all of the restaurants on the Via Portico d'Ottavia (the street lined with spots with outdoor tables); they're mostly touristic and mediocre (yes, even the famous ones that people mysteriously still rave about on TripAdvisor), and the only one I'd consider eating at again is BellaCarne, a kosher Roman-Mediterranean restaurant.

What sights could I see here? The ancient ruins around the Portico d'Ottavia, including the Theatre of Marcellus; the synagogue; Piazza Mattei; Crypta Balbi (a little-known museum with its own underground).

How much time do I need? You can walk from one end of the area to the other in about 15 minutes, but to properly explore, give yourself at least an hour or two. Add another hour if you'd like to see the synagogue.

Where should I eat? For meals, BellaCarne, Sora Margherita, Al Pompiere or Pane Vino e San Daniele (all in the Jewish Ghetto, which is very small), or walk into the Campo dei Fiori area (next section) to try Roscioli. For baked goods and sweets, Antico Forno Cordella (Ghetto) or cross over to Campo and try Antico Forno Roscioli. For wine, Bartaruga (Ghetto). For beer, cross into Campo for Open Baladin.

Other buckets you could add on from here: The heart of the *centro storico;* ancient Rome; Trastevere; the Forum Boarium.

Campo dei Fiori

This is not a *rione,* but I'm using this as shorthand to describe the whole area to the west and northwest of the Jewish Ghetto, but south of the Corso Vittorio Emanuele (the big street that cuts right through the center, from the river to Piazza Venezia). Although the square called Campo dei Fiori itself is always bustling, you still can find some streets and corners in this area that are Rome at its most atmospheric, with cobblestoned streets, artisanal shops and beautiful *palazzi.*

What should I keep in mind? The "sight" most travelers see here (and sometimes only that) is Campo itself, but if that's the case, you're missing most of what makes this area wonderful! The piazza is famed for its open-air market, but that's become – if not a tourist trap – at least a market frequented by more tourists than locals (which has had the unfortunate effect of, over time, closing down many of the mom-and-pop shops and replacing them with souvenir stalls). Campo isn't much better at night, when the market disappears and is replaced by hordes of young tourists, study abroad students, expats and the occasional Romans, drinking (often very significantly) at the square's pubs and bars. By all means see the square, but know that the best bits of this neighborhood are to be found outside of it. In fact, my favorite piazza in all of Rome is just a couple of streets behind it: Piazza Farnese.

What sights could I see here? Other than Campo dei Fiori, there is Piazza Farnese and beautiful Palazzo Farnese (if you want to go inside the palazzo, which is now the French embassy, you must book in advance; how to do so was outlined in the section on "Sights to book in advance"), Galleria Spada (not a must-see, but a fun way to see how paintings would have been shown in palaces in their heyday), the beautiful Via Giulia (possibly my favorite street in Rome, laid out by Pope Julius II more than 500 years ago) and the basilica of San Giovanni de' Fiorentini.

How much time do I need? If you don't go into any of the sights, which most people won't, but plan to just stroll and explore, one to two hours should give you a good overview of the area. Give yourself an extra hour for the Galleria Spada and an hour for Palazzo Farnese.

Where should I eat? For meals, Roscioli (between Jewish Ghetto and Campo dei Fiori), Ai Balestrari (Campo dei Fiori), Osteria la Quercia (Piazza Farnese), or Il Pagliaccio (very high-end – Via Giulia). For bakeries, Antico Forno Roscioli (between Jewish Ghetto and Campo dei Fiori), Forno Campo dei Fiori (Campo dei Fiori) or I Dolci di Nonna Vicenza (between Jewish Ghetto and Campo dei Fiori). For gelato, La Carapina (between Jewish Ghetto and Campo dei Fiori). For wine, L'Angolo Divino (Campo dei Fiori) or Enoteca Il Goccetto (Via Giulia). For beer, Open Baladin (between Jewish Ghetto and Campo dei Fiori). Remember that the Jewish Ghetto is just to the east and very compact so any of those spots will be convenient, as well.

Other buckets you could add on from here: Trastevere; Jewish Ghetto; the heart of the *centro storico;* the Forum Boarium.

Trastevere
The name means "Over the Tiber river", but don't let that fool

you: Trastevere is very much central. (In fact, if you walk from the synagogue and cross Tiber Island, you'll be there). It's well worth visiting for an afternoon or evening and has some excellent off-the-beaten-path sights to offer, including Raphael frescoes and ancient undergrounds.

What should I keep in mind? Although this is a lovely area and many locals do, of course, live here, guidebooks tend to overemphasize how "authentic" an area it is. While it remains an evocative *rione* of cobblestoned streets and hanging laundry, it also has become one of study-abroad programs, American universities and lots of tourists, particularly north of the Viale Trastevere, around the Basilica of Santa Maria in Trastevere. In the area south of the Viale Trastevere, it's a bit less packed. This area also gets crowded at night, particularly on weekends and in warmer weather, as the bars here are very popular with the under-30 set. Also remember that Trastevere's small churches are among its finest sights, but these often close between about 12:30pm and 4pm, so plan accordingly.

Finally, note that while there is a Trastevere train station, this is in a more residential area of Trastevere that is *not* normally the area tourists mean to visit, and is quite a walk from the sights – if you are coming from the center, you are better off taking the number 8 tram, which runs frequently and reliably from Piazza Venezia and Largo Argentina all the way through Trastevere.

What sights could I see here? The Church of San Crisogono (and its underground – more in the next section); the Church of Santa Cecilia in Trastevere (I consider this a must-see thanks to its underground ruins and Pietro Cavallini's Last Judgment; this is also mentioned next); the Basilica of Santa Maria in Trastevere, one of Rome's oldest churches and well worth a stop for its sparkling mosaics by Cavallini; the lavish, 16th-century Villa Farnesina, which has stunning frescoes by Raphael, Sodoma and Baldassare Peruzzi (keep in mind that the villa closes at 2pm); the art at Palazzo Corsini; and the Orto Botanico, a botanical garden run by the University of Rome.

How much time do I need? With its attraction being the

atmosphere more than any one specific site, this is an area to explore, not race through. Give yourself at least a couple of hours.

Where should I eat? For meals, Da Teo, Da Enzo dal 1929, Taverna Trilussa, Enoteca Ferrara and the pizzeria Ai Marmi, all in the center of Trastevere, or Hostaria Fernanda, closer to the Trastevere train station. For wine, Il Baretto or Enoteca Ferrara; for beer, Birrifugio or Ma Che Siete Venuti a Fa, in the center, or Luppolo Station, near the station; for drinks and aperitivo, Ny.Lon or Freni e Frizioni.

Other buckets you could add on from here: Jewish Ghetto; Testaccio/ Ostiense. You'll also be relatively close to the Janiculum hill – you can grab a bus or take the half-hour hike along Via Garibaldi, which winds up the hill to Piazza Garibaldi – which has beautiful, postcard-perfect views over the city of Rome, particularly at dusk.

Forum Boarium

I adore this tiny sliver of a neighborhood, tucked between the Roman Forum and Palatine hill. It also is so easy to get to and so manageable to explore that I think it deserves to be on the itinerary of any traveler who plans to stay for three or more days. Once a thriving part of ancient Rome as the city's cattle market (hence its name), it remains scattered with ancient ruins and monuments, as well as some of the loveliest churches in the city.

What should I keep in mind? Since most of the sightseeing here (and there isn't a great deal) is in small churches, make sure you visit in the morning or evening, as many tend to close in the afternoon. The weekend is one of the best times to visit, as on most Saturdays and Sundays you can find the local Campagna Amica food market open here.

What sights could I see here? The Church of San Giorgio in Velabro, a lovely 5th-century church with a 13th-century porch that was pieced together painstakingly after the Mafia bombings of 1993; the ancient arch next to the church, which dates to 264 A.D. and was a gate on the road between the main forum and Forum Boarium (note the wiped-off faces inside – they were once of Emperor Caracalla's brother, head of praetorian guard and wife, respectively, but all three fell out with him and were victims of *damnatio memoriae*, the convenient Roman process of wiping someone from the history books); the ancient Arch of Janus; the Temple of Hercules the Victor, in its newly-landscaped little green park on the river; the Church of San Nicola in Carcere, with its fantastic ancient ruins and underground (more in the next section); the Church of Santa Maria in Comedian, a lovely Romanesque church most famous for its Mouth of Truth; and Circus Maximus.

How much time do I need? Although this is a tiny area, it's packed with sights, so if you're planning to see them all, give yourself at least an hour and a half to enjoy.

Where should I eat? When the Campagna Amica market is open on weekends, it often has an area set up at the back where you can buy economical, tasty local food like sandwiches and sometimes hot meals and, when the weather is nice, eat outside on the terrace. For pastries and coffee, try Cristalli di Zucchero. Otherwise, cross into the Jewish Ghetto or Trastevere, just over the bridge.

Other buckets you could add on from here: The heart of the *centro storico*; Jewish Ghetto; Trastevere; Aventine.

Celio

This lovely green neighborhood is just west of the Colosseum. While some of its sights (like the Basilica of San Clemente) individually can be easily added on to the Ancient Rome bucket, if you have time, this is worth a dedicated bucket of its own. Though it is off the beaten path for most tourists, Celio is an ancient area that still has a remarkable number of sights.

What should I keep in mind? Like the Forum Boarium, much of the sightseeing here is in small churches, which tend to close from about 12pm to about 4pm, so make sure you visit in the morning or evening.

What sights should I see here? The Basilica of San Clemente (also written about in the Ancient Rome section); the basilica of Santi Quattro Coronati, with its medieval frescoes; the round church of Santo Stefano Rotondo; the Case Romane, ancient Roman apartments beneath the Basilica dei S.S. Giovanni e Paolo; the lovely little Celimontana park; the Baths of Caracalla. Many of these are my favorite sights in all of Rome, so there is more about them in the next section.

How much time do I need? To see all of the sights here, give yourself a half-day.

Where should I eat? You'll have more choices in the next neighborhood over, Monti, but if you don't want to leave Celio, try Li Rioni or Il Tajut for meals. For wine, DivinOstilia.

Other buckets you could add on from here: Ancient Rome; Appia Antica; San Giovanni.

Appia Antica

As an archaeological park surrounding the 2,300-year-old Appian Way, the Appia Antica isn't a single site, but a collection of them. The Appian Way (or, to Italians, Via Appia) was built all the way back in 312 B.C. And it was crucial. The first road linking farther-flung parts of the Roman empire with the capital, it first ran to Capua, just north of Naples; since it allowed Romans to transport soldiers and supplies, the Via Appia proved integral to the Romans conquering the Samnites of southern Italy. In 191 B.C., the Romans extended the road all the way to Brindisi, in modern-day Puglia.

That's the context. The really cool part? You can still walk on the Via Appia Antica today – on stones ancient Romans would have walked on. Some major events happened here, too. Spartacus, the famous leader of Rome's largest slave revolt, was crucified on the Via Appia along with 6,000 of his followers in 71 B.C.; St. Peter took this road out of Rome, fleeing Nero's persecutions, in 64 A.D. (according to the tale, this also is where he saw Christ – crucified years earlier – coming into the city as he left). In the villas along the road, early Christian converts allowed their fellow Christians to worship and, ultimately, to be buried beneath their gardens; catacombs sprung up along (and beneath) the Appian Way.

What should I keep in mind? Much of this area is pedestrian-only, which makes it perfect for a stroll. You also can rent bikes cheaply here and cycle, but beware – the paving stones can make it tough!

What sights should I see here? The Circus of Maxentius (once the second-largest circus in Rome, after the Circus Maximus); the 2nd-century Villa dei Quintili (the remains of a wealthy villa); the catacombs of St. Callixtus; catacombs of St. Sebastian; the Baths of Caracalla (also mentioned in the Celio section).

Where should I eat? There aren't many restaurants here, and the ones that are here are fairly touristic. The only one I'd recommend is Hostaria Antica Roma, which has the added benefit of having its own ancient columbarium. Other than that, consider taking a picnic or arranging to be elsewhere for main meals.

Other buckets you could add on from here: Celio; San Giovanni.

Aventine

Just over the Circus Maximus from the Forum Boarium is the Aventine hill. Like the Forum Boarium, what it lacks in size it makes up for in loveliness (in the spring, its bloom-laden trees and gardens make it one of the loveliest places for a stroll in Rome), and what it lacks in number of sights it makes up for with the quality of the handful it does have.

What should I keep in mind? The churches here close from about noon to 4pm, so time your visit accordingly.

What sights could I see here? Il Roseto di Roma, or the rose garden, is a botanical garden that's at its best in June, when the roses are blooming; Parco Savello, informally known as Giardino degli Aranci (Garden of the Oranges), has one of the most romantic views over the Tiber River; next door, the 5th-century Basilica of Santa Sabina is a gem; just down the street, the keyhole in the headquarters of the Order of the Knights of Malta is where you can get that view of the perfectly framed dome of St. Peter's Basilica, giving you three sovereign states – the Order of the Knights of Malta, Italy, and Vatican City – in one glance. (Yes, that's where this book cover came from!).

How much time do I need? You could walk from one side of the Aventine to the other in 20 minutes, but if you want to poke into the sights and enjoy your stroll, give yourself at least an hour.

Where should I eat? This area is more residences than restaurants, so you're better off heading down the hill to Testaccio or over the river to Trastevere.

Other buckets you could add on from here: Forum Boarium; Testaccio/Ostiense; Trastevere.

Testaccio/Ostiense

These two neighborhoods sit side-by-side just south of the city walls, and while they're quite different in character, they both provide a different view of Rome you're not likely to get if you stick to the area around the Pantheon and Colosseum.

In ancient times, Testaccio was the site of Rome's port – which explains the hill, Monte Testaccio, as it was formed by all of the broken amphorae dumped here after transporting olive oil. In the 19th century, Testaccio was the site of Rome's slaughterhouse. Despite its working-class roots, Testaccio today is a favorite area for young Romans to live, but still has a sizable community of old-timers, too – many of whom you can see going for surprisingly sprightly *passeggiate* in the Piazza di Santa Maria Liberatrice each evening. While Testaccio doesn't have a long list of must-see sights, it is becoming a more and more common destination for its food scene, meaning you're now likely to see something in this area you never would have before: small groups coming through the streets on food tours.

Meanwhile, Ostiense, just south of Testaccio, is a rare area where Rome feels both gritty and cool with its urban art, abandoned (and renovated) warehouses, and trendy bars. Unlike Testaccio, it remains frequented by few tourists and has even fewer sights to speak of, but for those interested in Rome's hip-gritty side, it's worth checking out.

What should I keep in mind? Don't expect cobblestoned streets, and know that the new Testaccio food market, which opened in 2012 in a clean, modern but soulless sprawl of a building, simply doesn't have the charm of the one that used to be here. If you want to visit the MACRO Testaccio, know that it has strange hours (currently from 2pm to 8pm), so double check its hours online before visiting.

What sights could I see here? The Pyramid, a 2,000-year-old tomb that looks straight out of Egypt (except for the travertine, anyway) which just was cleaned, restored and opened for pre-booked tours (as of 2017 in Italian only), on the border of Testaccio and Ostiense at the Pyramide metro station; the lovely Protestant Cemetery (home to Keats, Shelley, and other non-Catholic notables), also near the Piramide metro station; MACRO Testaccio, which puts on contemporary art exhibits in the slaughterhouse that gave the quarter its livelihood, in the heart of Testaccio; the food market in Testaccio; Centrale Montemartini, a unique museum of ancient Roman sculpture displayed in a renovated power plant, in Ostiense; the Basilica of St. Paul's Outside the Walls, one of Rome's five major basilicas and home to the tomb of St. Paul the Apostle, as well as a 5th-century arch mosaic and 13th-century cloisters (at the southern side of Ostiense).

How much time do I need? To walk around Testaccio and dip into a couple of the main sights, one to two hours. To visit Ostiense, particularly sights like Centrale Montemartini or St. Paul's Outside the Walls, another hour or two – but consider taking a bus down Via Ostiense to get there as the area is bigger than it seems.

Where should I eat? For meals, Flavio al Velavevodetto, Da Bucatino, the pizzeria Da Remo or Da Felice (Testaccio), or Porto Fluviale and Doppiozeroo (Ostiense); for a quick meal, Mordi e Vai, a stall selling incredible takeaway sandwiches in the Testaccio market; for coffee and *cornetto,* Café Barberini (Testaccio); for pastries, Sicilia e Duci (Testaccio); for beer and aperitivo, Oasi della Birra (Testaccio); for wine, Doppiozeroo (Ostiense).

Around Termini

The area around Termini train station, at the top of the Esquiline hill, isn't one of the prettier parts of Rome. It's one of the few places in the center where you'll see people roughing it on the streets, there's plenty of graffiti and the traffic, as you'd expect, is horrendous. I'm giving it its own bucket, though, because there are a number of sights in the area worth exploring – and which many people miss.

What should I keep in mind? The good thing about coming here is that it's incredibly easy to get to: Termini means "terminus", and the station here isn't just the terminus for many train lines into Rome, but also where metro lines A and B meet and where many buses reach the end (or start) of their line.

What sights should I see here? Palazzo Massimo, Rome's fantastic archaeological museum (also in the next section); the basilica of Santa Maria degli Angeli, which Michelangelo designed using the ancient baths of Diocletian; the Church of Santa Maria della Vittoria, with its extraordinary (and somewhat erotic) Bernini sculpture of Saint Teresa in ecstasy; Terme di Diocleziano, a national museum (on the same ticket as Palazzo Massimo) with inscriptions and sculpture, built into the ancient baths of Diocletian.

How much time do I need? For the main sights, including the museums, about three or four hours.

Where should I eat? For meals, Trattoria Morgana or Trattoria Monti. For wine, Trimani Wine Bar. For gelato, Come il Latte and I Caruso (two of my absolute favorite gelato spots in Rome).

Other buckets you could add on from here: Ancient Rome; heart of the *centro storico*.

More exploring

I'm including these buckets last not to imply that they are in any way inferior to those in the previous section. Rather, whether because they're slightly further afield or have fewer sights that most visitors are interested in, they're normally the kinds of areas people go to either for a specific purpose (like a particular restaurant), or when they have more than three or four days to play with.

These areas are fascinating and beautiful in their own right, though, so don't dismiss them. In particular, if it's your third or fourth trip to Rome – or if you're the kind of traveler who really enjoys getting off the beaten path and seeing truly local areas, even if it means having less time to "sightsee" – you may enjoy these.

Pigneto: Like Ostiense and Testaccio, this charming, working-class quarter has undergone a transformation in recent years: it's now one of the hippest areas in Rome. Despite being just west of Termini train station, it was also a little harder to get to, since it didn't have any metro stations – but that changed with the opening of a new Line C station there in 2015. With its buzzing pedestrian main street, cocktail bars and hip restaurants, it's one of Rome's prime spots for nightlife (not to mention the number-one hipster hangout).

San Lorenzo: Just north of Termini train station, this neighborhood has Communist roots and lots of university students, underground bars, graffiti and gritty music venues – as well as one of the loveliest churches in Rome, San Lorenzo fuori le Mura.

San Giovanni: This area, due east of the Colosseum and Celio and based around the ancient Roman walls, is visited mainly by pilgrims. That's because it happens to be the location of the Basilica of San Giovanni – the formal seat of the Pope – as well as the Scala Santa (Holy Stairs) and baptistry. It was here, too, that the Pope's palaces used to be, before moving to their current location after the Pope's return from Aquitaine at the end of the 14th century.

Parioli: North of the historic center, Parioli feels unlike much of the rest of Rome, with grid-patterned streets that feel more continental than Italian and elegant, upmarket *palazzi* and embassies. Parioli's Villa Ada is a particularly pretty park, and the catacombs of Santa Priscilla are an interesting stop.

Quarter Coppedè: It's technically in Parioli, but this quarter is a destination in itself. A neighborhood that was the fantasy of a single architect (his name: Coppedè) and built from the late 1910s until the late 1920s, this compact area is a charming mishmash of fantasy – every inch of its buildings has been painted, sculpted or designed with strange, charming details, whether a spiderweb or a musical notation, that make it the most whimsical area in Rome.

Garbatella: A bizarre, charming quarter just west of Ostiense which was planned as a suburb under Mussolini, but then taken over by Communists, who radicalized the neighborhood with hammer-and-sickle flags and red-painted walls. Today, the area has a worn-in charm and sense of character unlike any other quarter in Rome.

EUR: South of Ostiense, EUR (pronounced "*AY-or*") gets its name from its original purpose: Esposizione Universale Roma. The area was planned and built for Rome's hosting of the 1942 World Fair – which never happened, thanks to a little something known as World War II. The buildings are Fascist in every sense, including in how they reinterpret ancient Roman buildings. In a city whose tumbles of ruins and uneven streets can remind visitors of the messiness of humanity, the oddly immaculate, organized EUR couldn't be a more different experience.

Just a few of my favorite sights

I know I said back in the intro that this wasn't your typical guidebook. But it's hard for me to give you advice on Rome and *not* mention a few of my absolute favorite places to explore, particularly because many of them are the kinds of places that you might not know about unless you're a local – or on your third or fourth trip to Rome. If you read the previous sections on sights that you must book in advance and on how to organize your sightseeing, many of these names will look familiar. This, though, is where I want to tell you just a little bit more about them – and why for me, personally, they are "must-sees" of a different kind. I've organized them into different sections, according to what your interests might be: the underground (for those who love history, archaeology, or just want to see the city's hidden side), art (for lovers of beauty and art), and outdoor sights (for those who like combining sightseeing with fresh air!). Of course, many of these categories are necessarily mixed – an underground sight will have glorious frescoes, an art museum may specialize in ancient Rome, a park might be full of Roman ruins – so it's worth skimming all of them, no matter your interests. Finally, if the interest that inspires you most when you travel, is something not listed here, don't worry: We'll cover food and shopping later, while it goes without saying that absorbing the local culture and doing as Romans do doesn't need its own section; it underscores this whole book.

Do note that, again, these are just some ideas to get you started when it comes to off-the-beaten-path, top-notch sights in Rome. There are many, many more fantastic sights that I didn't include.

For everything listed here, please look online or, better yet, call to find out the hours and days of closure to avoid disappointment. (Again, some of these you also have to book in advance... which you know from earlier).

Underground Rome

Anywhere you go in Rome, you are walking on a buried, ancient world. Beneath your feet lie the remnants of the city that ruled an empire: Temples and streets, villas and churches, monuments and tombs.

Of course, this reality is not exclusive to Rome. Ground levels rise over time, a simple concept that underpins stratigraphy, one of modern archeology's main tenets. Rome's location in a valley next to a (frequently flooding) river, though, means that the ground level has risen particularly dramatically here – about 20-23ft (6-7m) since ancient times. That, combined with the fact that the city's "modern" burst of construction didn't occur in earnest until the 17th and 18th centuries, when the ruins were already half-buried, means that many of the older buildings were never razed completely (although Romans certainly helped themselves to their marbles and precious stones for their new churches and palaces). Often, the structures were used as the foundations for new buildings.

As a result, some of the city's finest, most fascinating historical sights and archaeological treasures are not the ones you see just walking along the street: They lie underground. In recent years, the city has opened up even more "new" (in fact, extremely old) sights. Here are some of my favorites. (Be aware that once these sights have been excavated and open to the air, never mind to the public, they disintegrate even faster, so be careful not to touch anything: Moisture speeds up the process.)

Domitian's Stadium

Rome's iconic Piazza Navona has a strange shape. One end has two 90-degree angles, while the other is rounded. This is not because the Renaissance designers decided to get creative. It is because the piazza was built into (and on top of) the 1st-century stadium of Emperor Domitian. Although the stadium had been partly excavated for years, it was not open to the public. Only visitors who knew to take a peek just outside the piazza's northern end, where a gaping hole revealed one of the massive arches looming up from the depths, caught a glimpse.

That changed in January, when the city opened the Stadio Domiziano museum. Although the €8 price is unusually steep – if you're on a budget, there are equally rewarding underground sites that are much cheaper – for history buffs or the simply curious, it's pretty cool to see more of the arches, pillars and statues that lay hidden for so long. *stadiodomiziano.com*

Palazzo Valentini

When the city opened up two excavated, Imperial-era villas that sat beneath a 16th-century building at the Roman Forum's edge in 2007, it didn't just make the site accessible to the public. It also made it historically accessible in a way I haven't seen anywhere else in Italy. An automated, but extremely well done (and surprisingly dramatic) tour takes you through the villas' remains, from bath complex to kitchen; the rooms are lit up to recreate what they would have looked like – with lasers "repairing" the mosaics, filling in the frescoes, even adding the sounds of water splashing and children laughing. The approach manages to come off as more refreshing than corny. The video midway through also gives an excellent overview of what all of Rome would have looked like in ancient times. The English slots fill up fast, so make sure to book as far in advance as possible (how to do so in the section "Sights to book in advance"). *palazzovalentini.it*

Crypta Balbi

It seems hardly anyone comes to what may be Rome's most underrated museum. Located a stone's throw from Largo Argentina, Crypta Balbi offers one of the most comprehensive takes at what the ancient city centre looked like and how it evolved. Its other major draw, though, is underground. The modest museum was built on the remains of the Theatre of Balbus, which dates back to 13 B.C., and access to one of its sections is included in the price of your ticket. While not the city's most exciting underground sight, it is just as spooky-feeling as you'd hope – and with what you learned from the exhibits above, it's much easier to make sense of how it fits into the fabric of ancient Rome. *archeoroma.beniculturali.it*

Domus Aurea

Also called the "Golden House of Nero", this site – one of the finest archaeological gems in a city thick with them – was closed for ages. It shut in 2005, and then reopened in 2007 but closed again almost immediately, and after heavy rains in 2010, a 645sqft (60sqm) section of the ceiling caved in. For a long time, it seemed that the site underground, which suffered from flooding and drainage issues, would never open to the public.

Why was that a travesty? Because the Golden House of Nero was one of the most opulent, extraordinary buildings of ancient Rome – and a surprising amount of it survives today. Constructed by Emperor Nero in 64 A.D., the palace sprawled across up to 300 acres (1.2sqkm) of land left empty by Rome's ravaging fire. (Yes, Nero was the "fiddled while Rome burned" guy. Although that part is an urban legend, you can't deny his, erm, ingeniousness in using the conveniently cleared land for his dream palace). According to Suetonius, the palace was coated with gold and adorned with gems and shells; the main banquet hall was circular and revolved day and night, like the heavens.

But as later emperors tried to erase all memory of the highly-unpopular Nero, the Domus Aurea was forgotten, buried underground and used as the foundation for other structures, including Trajan's baths, still on the Colle Oppio above. When it was rediscovered in the 15th century, Renaissance visitors included the artists Perugino, Ghirlandaio, and Raphael – all of whom were inspired by the palace's frescoes and decorations and whose resulting work helped shape the direction of the Renaissance.

Today? The palace may be a far cry from its gold-coated origins, but it remains breathtaking. Soaring stucco ceilings still have their original colors intact; lovely, detailed frescoes dot the walls. Visits to the stunning, atmospheric site only have become more cutting-edge in recent months with the addition of virtual-reality headsets on the archaeologist-led tours. You must book in advance; more information in the previous section "Sights to book in advance". *coopculture.it*

The Vatican necropolis

Not just for pilgrims, the tour of the necropolis beneath St. Peter's Basilica provides a fascinating look at what was once an above-ground cemetery for both Christians and pagans. Seeing the burials together, sometimes in the same family tomb, erases ideas of religion being black and white in the 1st and 2nd centuries. Many of the tombs retain their elaborate mosaic decoration and viewing the area said to hold the tomb of St. Peter is spine-tingling for anyone, not just Catholics. The number of visitors allowed into the tomb is limited, so you can only enter on a tour with an official Vatican guide (somewhat unfortunately, as the guides tend to be dry and have iffy English). Book in advance by e-mailing scavi@fsp.va. (More information on how to book in "Sights to book in advance").

Colosseum underground

Five years ago, the underground at the Colosseum opened to breathless excitement. Called the hypogeum, it consists of the tunnels and rooms where gladiators waited for their turns to do battle – a kind of backstage area, complete with the remnants of the elevators that brought the fighters to the arena, that gives you a better grasp of just how planned (and purposeful) the violence here really was. As with the Vatican necropolis, it can only be accessed on a tour (more information in "Sights to book in advance"). *coopculture.it*

Basilica of San Clemente

This used to be one of my absolute favorite sights in Rome (perhaps it helped that it was a stone's throw from my apartment). Over the years, though, this church has become too popular for its own good. It is often crowded with tourists, and at the end of 2015, they raised the ticket price for the underground from €5 to a stunning €10 (to put that in perspective, for €2 more you could visit the Colosseum, Palatine, *and* Forum). On top of that, while the ground level of the basilica is free to enter (as are all churches in Rome), a man at the door is confusing unwitting tourists by telling them the admission price applies even there.

I'm still including it, though, because while the cost is a shame, it has not changed the fact that the site is fascinating. This layer-cake of a church is a 12th-century basilica (with striking Byzantine apse mosaics; again, this level is free to enter)... built on top of a 4th-century basilica... built on top of ancient Roman ruins, including apartments and a pagan mithraeum (place of worship for members of the cult of Mithras). But don't race to the bottom: The middle level, the ancient basilica, features fascinating frescoes. Don't miss the 11th-century depiction of a tale of the pagan Sisinnius, with its rare example of not only written vernacular Italian, but, shall we say, colourful Italian: Painted on the fresco are Sisinnius' words *"Fili de le pute, traite!"* ("Come on, you sons of whores, pull!").

It can be a little confusing to figure out what is what on your own, so if you're already shelling out the €10 to enter, you might consider doing it as part of a tour or at least investing in a handbook to the basilica, which you can buy in advance on Amazon or buy (albeit for a higher price) in the church's gift shop. *basilicasanclemente.com*

San Nicola in Carcere

Aside from San Clemente, a number of other churches in Rome have undergrounds that are open to the public – often for just a couple of euros. My favorite is at this little church in the Forum Boarium, just around the corner from the Jewish Ghetto and a stone's throw from the inexplicably famous Mouth of Truth. Even from the outside, you can see how it was built directly into ancient structures: the temples of Hope, Juno and Janus, the oldest of which dates back to the 3rd century B.C. and whose columns the church uses as its own.

Unsurprisingly, the basement holds some secrets. You'll find both the temples' bases and the ancient Roman path that ran between them. The massive tufa stones might not look like much compared to, say, the mosaics of the Vatican necropolis, but they are 500 years older. The underground isn't very big – it will take you less than 15 minutes to visit, read the information, and see the whole thing – but because you're so likely to be alone, it provides an evocative experience. *060608.it*

Santa Cecilia in Trastevere

Built in the 9th century on the spot where St. Cecilia was martyred in the 3rd century, this church, located on the quieter side of Trastevere to the southeast of the Viale Trastevere, has a beautiful 9th-century mosaic, 13th-century frescoes by Pietro Cavallini and below-ground excavations of two ancient Roman houses. According to tradition, one of these is the house of the saint Cecilia herself, who was executed while still a girl; even if you don't quite buy it, it's worth visiting for a walk through the ancient homes, still with bits of floor mosaic intact. It also has a famous sculpture by Maderno of Cecilia's body as it was found, incorrupt, when exhumed in 1599. Not to mention one of the prettiest courtyards I've ever seen. *060608.it*

Church of San Crisogono

Little in the exterior of this 12th-century church in Trastevere sets it apart from Rome's other churches. This is a benefit. It keeps the tourists away – particularly because most don't know about its underground. Beneath San Crisogono lie the remains of the 5th-century church that existed on the site before, complete with 8th-century frescoes. *060608.it*

Art-lovers' Rome

One of the most extraordinary things about Rome is that art and sculpture, like ancient ruins, are everywhere. Beauty is woven into the fabric of the city. And while in other European cities, sculptures have been spirited away, off the streets and out of the elements, for their own safe-keeping, Rome has taken the opposite tack. These pieces often are allowed to remain. That isn't always great for the art, but it *is* wonderful for passersby and residents, who can experience some of the city's most beautiful pieces as they should be experienced – every day and *in situ*.

If that weren't enough, Rome also has its fair share of museums with fantastic works.

Here are some of my favorite places to go when I'm looking for an art fix.

Borghese Gallery

Probably the finest art collection in Rome, the gallery includes stunning sculptures and paintings by Bernini, Caravaggio, Raphael, and more. But it tends not to be on most first-time tourist itineraries – which is a shame.

If you're a lover of beauty (and of those planning a trip to Rome, who isn't?), the Borghese Gallery is a must-see. First, there is its location. The Villa Borghese (which, confusingly for English speakers, refers to the entire park around the museum, not just the museum itself) was laid out in the 17th century by Cardinal Scipione Borghese. It remains one of Rome's prettiest green spaces. The building, too, is a rare gem. Never used as a home, it was built with the express purpose of showing off Scipione's art collection. With art and architecture intertwined, taking in the collection itself is a pleasant, unified experience. Look above you, and frescoes echo the themes of the pieces beneath. Look before you, and ancient and 17th-century sculptures of the same subjects intermingle.

If there's any broad generalization you can make about the collection, it is that it was borne out of passion. Borghese was such an avid collector that he had Domenichino jailed so he could get his hands on Diana Hunting and sent henchmen to steal Raphael's Entombment from Perugia in the dead of night. His methods may not be commendable, but you have to admit the collection has some extraordinary masterpieces. I'm not embarrassed to say that the Borghese is the only place where I have been moved to tears by art.

The Baroque master Bernini was supported by the cardinal from an early age, and as a result, some of his earliest, most famous and mind-blowing pieces are here. These include the incredibly evocative Apollo and Daphne, then thought impossible to render in stone; the David, a self-portrait of the artist showing him as he takes on critics and, perhaps, even Michelangelo's own world-famous David; and the Rape of Proserpina, so realistic you can see how Pluto's fingers indent Proserpina's plush skin — and feel her fear as he carries her to the underworld. It's extraordinary to think that these are all made of marble.

But Bernini's not the only hotshot at the Borghese. Caravaggio, that 17th-century scofflaw who split his time between brawling, barfights and Baroque art, has gotten renewed attention in recent years with the 400th anniversary of his death. But at the Borghese, he's always been a big deal. Like Bernini, one of his earliest patrons was Scipione Borghese, and the villa has his Sick Bacchus, Boy with a Basket of Fruit, and Madonna of the Snakes, among other pieces.

That's not to mention the collection's pieces by Rubens. Raphael. Correggio. Lucas Cranach the Elder. The list keeps going.

Remember that, as the number of visitors who can enter at one time is (thankfully) limited, this is another one you must book in advance.

Palazzo Barberini

Although I prefer the collection in the Borghese Gallery, this museum comes in a close second. As a stunning art museum in a Renaissance palace, Palazzo Barberini, located on Piazza Barberini, is an oft-overlooked gem in the heart of the city.

The palace, which belonged to the powerful, papal Barberini clan, has some stunning pieces, most notably La Fornarina (Raphael's original portrait of his lover, the baker's daughter); a copy of Hans Holbein's famous portrait of King Henry VIII; and Caravaggio's frightening Judith Beheading Holofernes. And the ceiling fresco here by Pietro da Cortona is considered one of Rome's major Baroque masterpieces. A triumph of *trompe l'oeil*, it literally "tricks the eye" into thinking that the ceiling opens up to show the heavens and tumbling figures. But it's also a political piece, a tribute to the Barberini family – the powerful clan whose Maffeo Barberini became Pope Urban VIII (and started construction on the building).

For fans of Baroque architecture, meanwhile, the building alone merits a visit. Started in 1627-1633 by Carlo Maderno with his nephew Francesco Borromini, construction was handed over to Borromini and his soon-to-be-rival Bernini. Yes, *that* Bernini. Some of his sculptures are also inside. *barberinicorsini.org*

Church of San Luigi dei Francesi

It's hard not to fall in love with Caravaggio, whose intense lighting, almost photorealistic scenes and high drama suck in even those who don't normally consider themselves art lovers. Much of the turbulence and emotions on the canvas likely originated in his own life. A tortured soul who lost his family to the bubonic plague as a child, he was almost as well-known for his ability to cause trouble as for his genius. He was arrested three times for brawling and assault – once, particularly memorably, for throwing a plate of artichokes in a waiter's face – and in 1606 killed a man (some say over a game of tennis). But even as he was constantly fleeing from the authorities and will-wishers, first from Rome to Naples, then Malta, then Sicily, he produced extraordinary work.

One of the most extraordinary of them all is the cycle of three paintings of St. Matthew that Caravaggio did for the Church of San Luigi dei Francesi, just around the corner from the Piazza Navona. Although he'd already completed dozens of paintings, it was this commission – awarded when he was just 26 years old – that made him a star.

It wasn't just that the style, so naturalistic and emotive, was completely unlike the more staid, traditional works being done at the time. It was also that these paintings were extraordinarily controversial. In what would become Caravaggio's signature elements, instead of portraying the saint as superior to any human man, Matthew is shown as someone far more relatable, down to his bare feet. More controversially still, in the "Inspiration of St. Matthew" an angel is shown ticking off points that he wants Matthew to make in his revelations – a kind of divine intervention that's a little too direct, even though it was more subtle than Caravaggio's first version of the painting, which showed the angel whispering in Matthew's ear. (That version was rejected).

Today, even while many of those finer religious points are lost on most of those who look at the paintings, what is lost on no one is the dramatic perspective and lighting that makes you feel like you're in the paintings yourself, participating with the subjects. It's no wonder that this cycle thrust Caravaggio, as difficult of a person as he was, into the limelight as an artist. (If you head up the street to Santa Maria del Popolo, one of the churches on Piazza del Popolo, you'll find two more paintings by Caravaggio which are equally striking. These depict scenes from the lives of St. Peter and St. Paul). *060608.it*

Church of Santa Maria Sopra Minerva

Just behind the Pantheon, this is one of Rome's only Gothic churches, meaning it's in a completely different style (much more like Paris' Notre Dame than St. Peter's Basilica) than the rest. It has a sculpture said to be by Michelangelo (it was probably done mostly by one of his students, but with his help), lovely frescoes by the early Renaissance master Filippino Lippi (it's worth inserting coins into the slot to light these up, as otherwise they're quite dark), and the body of St. Catherine of Siena (her separated head, interestingly, is on display in the city of Siena). *santamariasopraminerva.it*

MAXXI

If you're looking for Rome's more modern side, then few places are better to visit than the MAXXI. Although it's out of the historic center, it is easy enough to get to: From Piazza del Popolo, you can jump on tram 2, which shoots straight up the Via Flaminia; a 10-minute ride brings you to a stop a five-minute walk from the museum. The stunning, enormous structure, designed by award-winning architect Zaha Hadid, provides a glimpse of a very different Rome than what you see if you stick to the Vatican, Colosseum (and even, for that matter, my beloved Borghese). The collection includes some of the best contemporary artists in the world and exhibitions that change throughout the year. *www.fondazionemaxxi.it*

Church of Santa Prassede

Lots of travelers visit the Basilica of Santa Maria Maggiore. Few know that just around the corner, Rome boasts an equally precious, way older – and, in my opinion, more moving – church. Just don't be swayed by its unassuming exterior.

The Basilica of Santa Prassede stands on the site of St. Prassede's own house where, according to tradition, she put up martyrs including St. Peter. A church was first built here in the 5th century, although an oratory might have existed as early as 150

A.D. The ruins of those earlier buildings haven't yet been excavated. But in the meantime, you can explore the current church – which was built in the 9th century.

The real reason to visit, though, is the art: Incredibly, the church still retains its frescoes and mosaics from the 9th century. The mosaics especially are extraordinary, covering the small Chapel of St. Zeno from floor to ceiling in glitter and gold. Don't forget coins to light the chapel up – you'll feel like you're inside of a Byzantine-era disco ball. *060608.it*

Basilica of Santi Quattro Coronati

A 12th-century church (with 4th-century origins) with a lovely cloister, this church and convent, in the same neighborhood as the Basilica of San Clemente, hides a secret: The beautifully-preserved 13th-century frescoes in the Chapel of St. Sylvester.

The first church here was founded in the 4th century. Its name, "four crowned saints", comes from its original dedication to the four soldiers who were martyred by Emperor Diocletian after they refused to sacrifice to a pagan god. But in 1084, the Normans burned the church to the ground during their sack of Rome. Pope Paschal II built the "new" version of Santi Quattro Coronati in the early 1100s, but at only half the size of the original. Still, the structure remains impressive, particularly for the lesson that the pope seems to have taken from the Norman sack: If you're going to build, might as well build fortified. Even today, Santi Quattro Coronati has the appearance, looming from atop the Celian hill and surrounded by thick walls, of a military fort.

There are two parts of the basilica that you shouldn't miss – but would if you didn't know what to look for. One is the Romanesque cloister. The other is the Chapel of St. Sylvester. Glorious but intimate, the chapel highlights the incredible narrative power of medieval frescoes, even those done by artists whose names have been forgotten. The 13th-century cycle of frescoes commemorates the life of St. Sylvester; the frescoes are charming (they hadn't quite figured out perspective yet!), but breathtaking, too. They're also incredibly rare for their state of preservation, giving you a chance to see 700-year-old frescoes largely as they're meant to be seen – vivid with color and detail. It's not all that often that you get to see medieval frescoes in Renaissance art-laden Rome. Especially not alone, as you're likely to be. Enjoy it.

To enter the chapel, ring the little bell on the left after you've walked in. A nun will appear behind the grate and ask how many you are. There's a small fee (a euro or two) per person. Once you've paid, she'll buzz you into the chapel. *060608.it*

Basilica of Santo Stefano Rotondo

It may look like a lovely, serene round church at first glance, but don't be fooled. This isn't a sight for those with weak stomachs.

Built on top of the remains of a 2nd-century Mithraic temple, the church was built in the 5th century A.D. to hold the body of Saint Stephen, which just had been brought to Rome from the Holy Land. The church's architecture is particularly unusual. As Rome's first circular church, it was modeled after Jerusalem's Church of the Holy Sepulchre.

While that round shape makes it an architectural delight, the other draw is its frescoes. Spiraling around the circular walls, the paintings depict 34 different martyrs – each being killed in gruesome ways. Molten lead poured down the throat? Check. Breasts cut off? Check. Boiled alive? Check! Commissioned by Pope Gregory XIII near the end of the 16th century, the paintings are naturalistic in their graphic displays, making anyone who looks closely enough wince. The peaceful expressions on most of the martyrs' faces go somewhat toward mitigating the "ouch ouch OUCH" effect... although in all honesty, that eerie calm seems a bit more disturbing than convincing. If you're horrified by the frescoes, by the way, you're in good company: Charles Dickens wrote after his visit that the church displayed "such a panorama of horror and butchery no man could imagine." You've been warned. *santo-stefano-rotondo.it*

Palazzo Massimo

Although often referred to as Rome's main "archaeological museum", Palazzo Massimo, located a stone's throw from Termini station, is more accurately an art museum – where all of the art in it happens to be ancient. (It's also true that if you haven't been to Palazzo Massimo, then you haven't seen the best of Rome's archaeological finds).

At this museum around the corner from the Termini train station, you'll find some of Rome's most famous bronze and marble sculptures – and then some. Treasures like ancient mosaics. Elaborately-carved sarcophagi. Incredibly-preserved frescoes taken from some of Rome's most opulent ancient villas. Even the super-cool Fasti Praenestini, an enormous marble calendar set up in the forum of a nearby town.

Some of the art is so famous, you'll recognize it from postcards, book covers or even your university art history class – like the 1st-century B.C. bronze The Boxer, slumped with weariness after his (unsuccessful?) match, or ancient Roman copies of the 5th-century B.C. Discobolus (that super-classical athlete tossing a disc).

The real reason to go to Palazzo Massimo, though, is its ancient fresco collection. Not just because it's fantastic, but because the museum has a whole section devoted to the Villa of Livia, Augustus' wife. Better yet, it's set up like the villa itself so you can actually see how the rooms would have looked, complete not just with the frescoes on the walls, but delicate, detailed molding on the ceiling and mosaics on the floors. Amazingly, hardly anyone tends to come here. *archeoroma.beniculturali.it*

Palazzo Farnese

Just behind bustling, increasingly-touristy Campo dei Fiori is Piazza Farnese, my favorite piazza in Rome. It's graceful, gorgeous, and quiet. And much of the atmosphere here comes from *Palazzo* Farnese, built in the 16th century by the powerful Farnese family (one of the architects was Michelangelo) and, today, the French embassy. Tours of the palace's interior are now offered in English, and since it's the only way to see the inside – which includes one of the most magnificent works of the High Renaissance, a monumental fresco cycle by Annibale Carracci – it's worth doing. The tour must be booked in advance (more in "Sights to book in advance").

Villa Farnesina

If you liked the Raphael rooms in the Vatican, then pay a visit to this lovely villa, located in the heart of Trastevere. Raphael produced some of his most famous frescoes here (at the same time, the story goes, as he was seducing the daughter of a local baker, the famous La Fornarina of the painting now in Palazzo Barberini). Other artists with works in the villa include Giulio Romano and Sodoma.

Rome's outdoors

From the Forum to Palatine to Trevi Fountain, many of Rome's most famous sights are outdoors. If that appeals to you – and in Rome, where the weather is lovely 90% of the time, it should – here are some other suggestions you may not have thought of. (These are, of course, also good with children).

Villa Borghese

I wrote under the art-lovers' section about the Borghese Gallery, but the estate that the museum is in, considered Rome's answer to Central Park, is worth a stop as well.

Though on a map it may look far away, it's not. You can get there easily from the top of the Spanish Steps or by climbing up the Pincian hill at Piazza del Popolo. The park is just the right size to feel like you've gotten out of the city, but not so big you'll get lost (or die of exhaustion if you're jogging around it in a loop), and with umbrella pines, ancient-looking follies and a tiny pond, not to mention several other museums, there's plenty there to enjoy. As there also are often people putting on street shows for children, as well as a carousel, a pond where you can rent rowboats and places to rent those funny four-wheeled cycling carts, it's also a great place to take children.

Baths of Caracalla

If you want to get a real idea of the *enormity* of ancient Rome, then come here. The remains of the 3rd-century baths tower 125ft (38m) above you, higher than many of the apartment complexes of modern-day Rome; they once accommodated up to 1,600 people at a time. Today, however, there's hardly anyone there.

The baths (or *terme*, in Italian) date back to the early 200s A.D., when they were planned by Emperor Septimus Severus and completed by his son Caracalla. They boasted a 183-by-79ft (56-by-24m) frigidarium, tepidarium, 115ft-wide (35m) caldarium, natatio (swimming pool) complete with bronze mirrors to reflect in the sunlight, and two palaestras, or gyms. And that's not to mention the complex's dozens of shops and two public libraries – one with texts in Latin, one in Greek.

There's little left of the opulent mosaics and statues that once studded these spaces, but the sheer size alone will take your breath away. *archeoroma.beniculturali.it*

Giardino degli Aranci

I include the "Garden of the Oranges", more properly called the Parco Savello, for a few reasons. It has a gorgeous view of Rome. There are indeed orange trees, and ones with a history – they're said to be the first orange trees brought to Italy by none other than St. Dominic himself.

Coming here gives you an excuse to explore the Aventine hill, with its graceful buildings and many ancient treasures. But, more than that, it is one of Rome's loveliest and most romantic parks. (I have proof of the latter claim: When someone recently reached out to me via the Revealed Rome Facebook page asking where he should propose to his girlfriend in Rome, I said there or the Janiculum. He sent me a photo a couple of days later with the caption: "It worked!").

Appia Antica

I made Appia Antica a "bucket" of its own in the previous

section, so I won't say too much more about it now. But it's worth noting that if you're interested in getting outdoors while exploring ancient Rome, or visiting a part of Rome that feels bizarrely like the countryside, then spending at least a half a day here is in order. *parcoappiaantica.it*

Scheduling your sightseeing in Rome

When organizing your itinerary in Rome – even if you're just getting a rough idea of what to see when – there's one thing to keep in mind: Not everything is open every day. The Vatican museums and Sistine Chapel close one day a week; so do many favorite restaurants and shops. Because everything is more fun with a (not-really-rhyming) rhyme, indulge me in the following...

Dreaming of the Sistine Chapel? Then don't go on a Sunday!

The Vatican museums (which include the Sistine Chapel) are open every day but Sunday. The last Sunday of the month is the exception, as they are open and free. But it's not something I recommend if you value your vacation time; the line is often three hours or more (and you can't book a ticket for these free Sundays in advance on the Vatican website). St. Peter's Basilica, though, is open daily; on Sunday, the Pope appears at 12pm to an audience on the square, and on Wednesday, he has his general audience at 10:30am.

Best time to go: Wednesday morning, as the museums tend to be emptier while the Pope does his audience; otherwise, Tuesdays, Thursdays or Fridays, since Saturday and Monday tend to be crowded with people who would have gone on Sunday.

And stay away from smaller churches – at least if it is midday

Most churches are open daily in Rome. However, many of the smaller, more off-the-beaten-path churches – which also, in my opinion, tend to be among Rome's loveliest sights – also close at midday, some for as long as from 12pm to 4pm. Always check in advance. On Sunday, remember that while they are open, they may be holding Mass and more ceremonies than usual, which can make it more difficult (or forbidden) for tourists to walk around to sightsee.

Best time to go: Morning or evening, except for Sundays (unless you want to attend Mass).

On Monday, many museums are a no-go...

Many of Rome's museums close on Mondays, but are open every other day of the week. These include the Borghese Gallery, Palazzo Barberini, Palazzo Massimo, Crypta Balbi, MAXXI, Castel Sant'Angelo, and the National Gallery of Modern Art (though not, as previously noted, the Vatican museums).

Best time to go: Tuesday through Friday; weekends tend to be more crowded than weekdays (not that that's much of a problem at some of these little-visited places, like the Crypta Balbi).

While for lots of restaurants, it's the day of *riposo*!

Most of Rome's restaurants have one "day of rest", even though this is no longer government-mandated. This day is typically – but not always – Monday, and sometimes Sunday for lunch and/or dinner as well (particularly for restaurants that are more elegant or upscale; since Sunday is a big pizza night, though, pizzerias are usually open Sunday). Some restaurants, like the popular Da Francesco near Piazza Navona, close Tuesday instead.

Best time to show up if you didn't make a reservation: Wednesday or Thursday (though increasingly, Rome's better spots are becoming booked up in advance even on these nights). Almost everywhere that's any good will have a wait or simply be unable to take you on Friday or Saturday nights, and if you're heading somewhere on a Monday, you'll want to call in advance (or look it up) to make sure they're open.

There is a catacomb open every day (phew)

Luckily, no matter what day you're planning on visiting the

catacombs, at least *one* will be open. Just make sure it's the right one! The catacombs of St. Sebastian and St. Agnes close on Sunday (St. Agnes also usually closed for the month of November), Santa Priscilla closes Monday, St. Domitilla closes Tuesday, and St. Callixtus closes Wednesday (as well as for a month during the winter, usually from late January to late February). The catacombs also close on most major holidays, and all but St. Sebastian also close over the lunch hour (usually from 12pm to 2pm), so double-check the hours on the websites.

Best time to visit the catacombs: When they're open, of course – and not on the weekend, which tends to be more crowded.

And the Colosseum and Forum are open daily, too

Most of Rome's most famous ancient sights are open daily, including the Colosseum, Forum, Palatine, and Pantheon (although the Pantheon does close slightly earlier on Sundays, at 6pm rather than 7:30pm). The Baths of Caracalla also open daily (but close at 2pm on Mondays, with last entrance at 1pm). They do, however, close on some major holidays, like Christmas, so double-check for those dates.

Best time to go to the ancient sites: Anytime – although to avoid lines and crowds at the Colosseum and forum, opt to either be there *first thing* in the morning (i.e. 8:30am), or later in the day (many people clear out by 3pm). Keep in mind if you're opting later, though, that the opening hours of the Colosseum, Palatine and Forum change according to the season (depending on hours of daylight), so in mid-winter, they close as early as 4:30pm.

Shops can be tough on Sunday, unless they're big and new

Shops in the heart of Rome's center – particularly on Via del Corso, around Piazza Navona, and near major sights – are open every day. Especially the chains. (More on why you *shouldn't* waste your time on those, though, later). Smaller shops, which often don't have the staff to open daily, tend to close one day a week; for many, this is Sunday. Lots of them stay closed through Monday morning.

Many of these smaller stores also close midday, like the smaller churches.

Best time to go shopping: Monday through Saturday, outside of lunchtime; to avoid shopping crowds in high-trafficked areas, try not to shop in the evening or on weekends.

Last-minute ways to skip the lines

Perhaps you missed the section on sights to book in advance. Perhaps you didn't want to commit to a certain date or time. Perhaps you just thought you'd try your luck. For whatever reason, you've now shown up at the Colosseum, Vatican museums or St. Peter's Basilica… and, thanks to the long line you see stretching out before you, regretted not buying a ticket earlier.

While there isn't any foolproof option left at this stage, you can, at least, cut down your waiting time if you know certain tricks.

Before I walk you through these options, though, I want to introduce you to one way to skip the line that you shouldn't resort to using: The sold-on-the-street, skip-the-line tour. (If you need a refresher on why, go back to the section "The most popular scams in Rome"). In short, you have no control over the quality of the guide (who won't normally be the person who sold you the tour), you often have to wait for a long time for the tour to start, you're frequently in a huge group, you're sometimes just muscled in front of other people waiting in line, and many of these operators are working illegally.

As you know from earlier, there are major benefits to taking tours of some of Rome's sites. But regarding these on-the-fly tours, consider yourself warned.

Now, onto less stressful, more reliable ways to skip the lines at…:

The Colosseum

If you've forgotten to do anything else in advance – and you don't want to, or can't, buy a ticket for later in the week online – then at *least* do this. When you want to go to the Colosseum, don't.

Instead, stop at the Forum entrance and ticket office on Via dei Fori Imperiali, or at the Palatine hill entrance and ticket office to the south of the Colosseum. Any Colosseum ticket is actually a *combined* Colosseum/Forum/Palatine ticket, which means you can get buy it at either of those spots, too. While there tend to be lines at those offices during high season, particularly in the mid-morning, they still will be much shorter than the line you see at the Colosseum.

The Vatican museums

Again, this will only cut down on your waiting time, not get rid of it altogether. But if you're planning to try to go to the Vatican museums without a ticket, then the trick is timing. If you can choose the day of your visit, opt for a Tuesday, Wednesday, or Thursday. Equally important, do *not* come in the morning. (Despite how large they are, it is unlikely you'll spend your entire day in the museums, anyway; most people get exhausted and hungry long before that). Instead, arrive shortly after or during lunch at about 1pm or 2pm. This should give you enough time to see all of the main sights – and because tour buses, cruise ship groups and many travelers come in the morning, it means the line will be shorter, and the museums less crowded, than they were at 9am or 10am. The later in the day you come, the shorter the line will be. (Just keep an eye on your timing when you're inside). This trick works especially well in the low season – November through February, outside of holidays – and, as you'd expect, gets less foolproof the closer you are to high season.

St. Peter's Basilica

There actually aren't tickets for St. Peter's Basilica (it's free to visit), so the long line you see at St. Peter's Square isn't for an entrance fee; it's for security. It does get long, though, so you'll still want to plot your strategy.

One good trick is to come either in the very early morning, or at the end of the day.

In the summer, from April 1 to September 30, the basilica is open from 7am to 7pm; in winter, from October 1 to March 31, from 7am to 6pm. Even in high season, if you arrive by 8am or come in the evening – around 5pm or 5:30pm – you'll often find there's often hardly any line at all. Just remember that, if you want to climb the dome, it's open from 8am to 4:45pm in winter and 8am to 6pm in summer.

Another option is to enter the basilica through the Vatican museums: There is an alternate exit from the Sistine Chapel that leads directly onto the porch of St. Peter's Basilica. Because anyone in the Sistine Chapel already has gone through the Vatican museums security check, there's no second check there. It is, however, meant to be an exit for tour guides and their groups only. Sometimes this isn't enforced, sometimes it is, and sometimes you can sneak onto another group and look like you're exiting together. Either way, it's a trick that isn't foolproof, but when it works, you'll feel very savvy indeed.

The bare necessities

When sightseeing in Rome, two basic needs are likely to come up. Needing water… and needing the bathroom.

Here's what you need to know.

Water in Rome

When you get thirsty in Rome, the really good news is that water is *everywhere.*

Seriously. Forget dragging around a 5-gallon Nalgene with you all day that you filled up at your hotel that morning. It's just not necessary. Water's all around you.

If you didn't bring your own water bottle, then grab one at one of Rome's many cafés. At a local, non-touristy café, a small bottle of water shouldn't cost any more than €.80; at a café right near a touristy spot, it can be up to €3. (And *never* buy a bottle of water, or anything else, for that matter, from one of the makeshift stands near the Colosseum or Vatican – unless you want to pay a pretty penny). The cheapest place to buy individual bottles of water, though, is almost always a grocery store.

But here's the trick: Once you've finished your bottle of water… don't throw it out! Instead, refill your bottle at one of Rome's more than 2,500 *nasoni* ("nah-ZONE-eeh"). This little fountains, named after their nose-shaped spigots, are everywhere. You might notice them because their water just runs and runs, with no need to turn them on or off. And yes, that water is perfectly safe to drink. Since the ancient times, Rome has provided its citizens with plentiful, clean water. In the 1st century A.D., thanks to the aqueducts, the city had 1,000 liters of water available per person, per day. Now, there are 500 liters available… per family. Still, more than enough.

Even today, the water is still brought in from outside the city. As well as being safe to drink, it's fresh. And super-cold.

One last tip: If you plug up the end of the spigot with your thumb, the water will spurt out of a handy hole on the top, providing you a makeshift water fountain – a good option if you accidentally threw out that water bottle.

Bathrooms in Rome

So you had success with tracking down, and drinking, all that water. Now, you need the restroom.

Rome isn't an amusement park or a shopping mall: There aren't public restrooms that people can just wander in to use. But you do have other options.

For one, every museum and major sight (including the Colosseum) has its own toilets. (Although brace yourself for the Vatican museums, because it's often a long walk between restrooms). If you're wandering around the city and find yourself in need, though, that's not so helpful.

Instead, this is the time to get a coffee.

You don't need a coffee? Maybe someone else in your group does. Or maybe you can buy a *tramezzino* (little sandwich). Or a pack of gum. Or another bottle of water.

There is a café on every corner in Rome, but to use the toilet, you need to become a customer first. (It's only polite). When you walk in, it's perfectly fine to ask if there's a bathroom and then indicate that you'll buy something after you use it. It's also good to ask since not every café actually has a toilet. And no, I have no idea where those particular workers go when nature calls.

Keep in mind that cafés in Rome often have a sign hanging outside that reads "BAR". This doesn't mean a bar serving alcohol; it means a coffee bar. Whether you need coffee or the toilet, that's the sign to look for.

Before moving on to less scatological topics, a final note. Not every restroom in Rome is stocked with the conveniences you'd assume. Particularly in cafés, bars, and clubs, bathrooms often lack soap (ew), toilet paper (yuck) or even a toilet seat (what?). So Italian women – and prepared travelers – usually stash a package of tissues in their purses, along with hand sanitizer, just in case. And yes, they become very good at hovering.

Sightseeing... sustainably

I wouldn't be a responsible guide to your visit to Rome if I didn't include this section.

As you'll see first-hand when you're here, not all tourism to Rome is benefiting Rome. Just take the fact that 20,000 people are visiting the Sistine Chapel every *day*, damaging the frescoes just a few years after their restoration. The Sistine Chapel is just the tip of the iceberg. Across Rome and Italy, frescoes are crumbling from walls and ruins are collapsing. Literally.

A lot of that, of course, has to do with lack of upkeep and proper preservation initiatives. But some of it also has to do with too many people in too few areas, especially when they're not aware of proper precautions like not touching artwork.

Want to help keep Rome's incredible cultural heritage intact so that you can appreciate it on a later visit – and so your children and grandchildren can, too? So do I. Here are some easy things we can all do (or avoid doing) to help.

Never, ever, ever touch the artwork

One of the best ways to ruin frescoes is to touch them – or even stand close to them, since humidity from your breath can help damage the delicate artwork. Similarly, never touch any paintings, sculptures, or even those sturdy-looking ancient ruins or bits and pieces you see lying around the Forum, Palatine, or anywhere else. If you break something, you'll feel very silly indeed.

Double-check before you snap a photo, especially with flash

Taking pictures isn't always allowed. And sometimes, even where it is allowed, it's bad for whatever your subject is. Never, for example, use flash photography on tapestries or cloth. And taking flash photos in some settings, like at Mass, is disrespectful. When in doubt, keep the camera off... and spend that time fixing what you're looking at in your memory instead of your memory card.

Go off the beaten path

Instead of being one of the crowd, seek out the lesser-known archaeological sights and museums. Not only are these the places that need tourist dollars more, but they also need awareness: The more word spreads about how cool they are, the more likely the government is to invest in them. (Hopefully).

Delve into what you're seeing

Learning as much as you can about what you're seeing makes your experience more rich and rewarding. It also helps the site itself. The more travelers really appreciate Rome's sights and the history behind them, especially for the off-the-beaten-path gems, the more Romans and the Italian government will be encouraged to protect and invest in those areas.

Put a coin in the box

Many of Rome's top sights charge admission. Others do not. That includes Rome's churches, which aren't just holy places –

they're full of art, sculpture, even ancient ruins. Many of them badly need money for restoration. If you liked what you saw, drop some coins in the donation box on your way out.

Stop at the museum gift shop

Why not grab a souvenir at a museum gift shop, rather than a store that imports cheap, plastic goods from overseas? A beautiful coffee-table book of the museum's paintings or a print will remind you of your visit again and again – and the funds help the museum, too.

Be an ambassador for Rome's heritage

Even when you're back home, you can spread the word about Rome's many gems and how they deserve to be protected.

Walk between the sights

As I've said before, walking is the best way to see Rome – as well as the only way to see those undiscovered corners and little gems that make Rome so special. Of course, it also happens to be the best for Rome's environment and for its Renaissance palaces and ancient ruins alike; few things are worse for these structures than pollution.

Give back

Increasingly, Italy is providing ways for people around the world to become involved in the restoration and upkeep of some of its most treasured sights. And while donation is always an option, there are more creative ways, too – from hands-on volunteering to opting to have a wedding or party at one of the properties.

FAI (fai-international.org), Italy's national trust, restores and maintains dozens of sights of cultural and natural heritage across Italy, including castles, gardens and abbeys. You can donate, volunteer, adopt anything from a tree to a restoration, or even opt to have a wedding or other event at one of their stunning sites.

Founded in 2014, the nonprofit LoveItaly (loveitaly.org) crowd-funds for a variety of restoration and archaeological projects, communicating where the costs come from and how they're spent in a clear, transparent way. In 2017, these included raising money for an important excavation of Rome's Palatine hill (the project's university funding dried up) and a much-needed restoration of the ancient House of the Centaur at Pompeii. (In return, sweeteners include gifts like a night's stay on Capri and a private tour of the Palatine excavation).

The Domus Aurea, which you know from earlier is extraordinary and which requires a €31 million restoration, is also at the center of a crowdfunding campaign you can donate to online.

The American Institute for Roman Culture (romanculture.org) increases awareness and campaigns to protect Rome's cultural heritage. Their specific projects have included petitions to save Hadrian's villa and the tomb of the gladiator, using social media to teach the world about ancient Rome, and running field excavation schools to inspire new generations of students, classicists and archaeologists. In fact, I feel so strongly about their work that for the re-launch of this book, I gave €1/$1/£1 for each e-book sold to AIRC in the first three months. I've enjoyed Rome's heritage – I want to be a part of protecting it.

Chapter 6
When in Rome

Eating

If you're – how do I put this – not crazy, you're probably excited to eat in Rome.

And you should be. The cuisine is one of the delights of spending time here. But before enjoying Rome's food, you have to wipe one misconception from your mind: You *can't* eat anywhere in Rome and still have a great meal.

It is sad, but true. Rome – like any other touristy city, including Paris, London, Madrid, and New York – is thick on the ground with mediocre, overpriced dining options.

In this section, therefore, I'll guide you through how to make the most of your limited time (and budget!) eating and drinking in Rome. This section includes:

•basic tips for picking a restaurant

•traditional Roman dishes to try

•how to eat if you are vegetarian, vegan, gluten-free or have another requirement

•which foods to order in which seasons
•etiquette mistakes not to make when eating in Italy
•everything you need to know about coffee… and gelato
•how to handle tipping
•how not to get ripped off eating in Rome
•my top choices for meals, gelato, coffee, wine and food markets

Six tips for eating well in Rome

To eat at the very best restaurants in Rome, it's always advisable to have a list of recommendations with you (and to make reservations in advance).

But what if you just want to eat well, avoid Rome's *worst* restaurants, and not spend tons of time researching and booking places to eat? Then at the very least, keep these six rules in mind.

1) Get away from the uber-tourist centers...

Or at least be aware that the closest you are to, say, the Colosseum, Vatican, or Trevi Fountain, the harder it'll be for you to find top-notch nosh.

2) Run, don't walk, away from that oh-so-friendly host trying to get you to come inside

He seems nice? He speaks English? He's telling you you're beautiful and your husband is a lucky man? That all means one thing: His food's not good enough for people – most notably Italians – to come in on their own. Beware!

3) A tourist menu signals danger

If you see something like "TOURIST MENU: 10 Euros for appetizer, pasta, and wine!" on the door or window, you're probably in trouble. Don't make the mistake of thinking you will, at least, save money; many of these "budget" menus sting you elsewhere, like on the cost of water, cover, or a service charge.

4) But an English menu doesn't

If you're handed a menu when you sit down and it's in English, don't worry. Lots of restaurants have them these days.

5) Never look for a place to eat at 6pm

Or 7pm. Or anytime before 8pm. As a general rule of thumb, if it's open that early, it'll be catering to tourists: Romans rarely eat before 8 or 8:30pm, and 9pm is the most usual time for dinner.

6) *Trattoria, osteria, taverna...meh*

Any difference there once was between these has pretty much slipped away. Just remember that a *birreria* is more a place for fried food and beer, and that most good *pizzerias* aren't open at lunch.

Keep your end goal in mind: That hole-in-the-wall place that doesn't even look like a restaurant on the outside, but when you walk in (at 9pm, remember), it's bustling with Italians. Eat only at gems like these, and you're guaranteed to have some of the best food in Rome.

Ciao, cucina romana!

Food culture in Italy is highly regional. Particularly at local, non-touristy restaurants, you won't find the same cuisine in Rome that you would in Bologna, Florence, or Venice. In Rome, or at least at traditional Roman restaurants, for example, you won't find risotto (which is associated with Milan and the north) or thick-crust pizza (which you'll find more in Naples and the south).

While that has downsides, I tend to think it's pretty cool. It makes the experience of traveling around Italy even richer and more rewarding. It allows you to connect in another way with the local community. It helps provide that the food you eat is made in a way that's been time-tested by the same locals who now are serving it to you. And it helps to ensure that the ingredients used are fresh and local, not imported from abroad.

Here are some basics to know about Roman (and not-Roman!)

food.

An introduction to Roman cuisine

Traditionally, Rome's food is known for being simple, in a good way. Most dishes use just a few, high-quality ingredients. *Carbonara* the authentic Roman way, for example, doesn't use cream, parsley or any of the other add-ons you sometimes find abroad – the sauce is simply fresh eggs, *guanciale* (pork jowl), salt and fresh-ground black pepper.

Also know that, while thin-crust pizza and some kinds of pasta are especially Roman, it's not all pizza and pasta here. Certain meat and fish dishes are also traditional, and are usually made, as per the "keep it simple, stupid" rule that governs Rome food, with little to no sauces.

Finally, more adventurous of eaters might want to explore Rome's *quinto quarto* cuisine. This refers to the part of the animal left over after the more-desirable parts were chopped up and sold. In other words, it's offal. *Trippa* (tripe), *coda alla vaccinara* (oxtail), and *cervelli* (brains) are all part of this tradition.

When in Rome, here are some dishes to try.

Bruschetta

Perhaps it was first invented in Tuscany, perhaps in Rome. Either way, *bruschetta* is a staple on the menu of most Roman restaurants. A very simple dish, it's said that it came about when 15th-century olive oil makers would toast their bread over a fire that they used to keep warm in the winter, then would taste-test their own olive oil on it.

Today, the recipe is pretty much the same: A good bread, rubbed with only a bit of garlic (this is *not* garlic bread... which doesn't exist in Italy!), and topped with olive oil. One of the most popular varieties, of course, is *bruschetta al pomodoro* (with tomatoes).

Just make sure you pronounce it correctly. It's "broo-SKETT-ah," not "broo-shet-ah".

Pecorino romano

Lazio's answer to *parmigiano-reggiano*, *pecorino* is a cheese made from sheep's milk (the name comes from *pecora*, meaning "sheep"). Hard, salty, and delicious, D.O.P.-protected *pecorino* is the staple of many Roman pasta dishes, and what you'll often be offered instead of *parmigiano*.

Carciofi alla giudia

Roman artichokes, or *carciofi romaneschi*, are world-famous. (Just remember that they're only in season from February to May. Outside of those months, any artichokes you see on the menu aren't the traditional Roman version. More about what's in season, when, and why that is important, later).

There are two classic ways to cook Roman artichokes. This way, meaning "Jewish artichokes," is a recipe from Rome's ancient Jewish community; it involves frying artichokes to a delicious crisp. Then there's...

Carciofi alla romana

Here, artichokes are slow-cooked so they're buttery and tender. Even if you don't like artichokes, try one of these two types. I promise they're not like the artichokes back home.

Fiori di zucca

These are "zucchini flowers", and they show up in Roman cuisine in all different ways; some pastas will even incorporate them. The most popular (and traditional) way, though, is on the *fritti* menu, where they're typically eaten before the meal. That's when they'll be stuffed with mozzarella cheese, usually an anchovy or two, and deep-fried.

Fave al guanciale

You'll often see *fave*, or fava (broad) beans, on Roman menus. Only order them when they're in season – the spring. In this popular *contorno* (side dish), they're served with *guanciale*, or pork jowl.

Puntarelle

Another typical Roman *contorno* or *antipasto* that should be served (and eaten) only when it's in season, from November through February. These crunchy green chicory shoots are served as a salad, dressed with olive oil, vinegar, anchovies and garlic.

Baccalà

A codfish, you see this prepared many ways in Rome. If you see it on the *fritti* menu, then the fish is served up fried – either as a popular antipasto or a *contorno* with some pizza.

Pizza

Of course, you can get pizza Italy-wide, but Roman pizza is among the best. Don't expect thick, fluffy pizza here; instead, Roman pizza is thin, crisp, and *always* baked in a wood oven.

Gnocchi alla romana

Usually served on Thursdays, these soft, tasty dumplings are made of semolina and served in sauce.

Bucatini

Meaning "little hole", this is a long pasta, slightly thicker than spaghetti. And yes, it has a (tiny) hole in the center. You can find dozens of varieties of pasta around Italy, but *bucatini* is most closely associated with Rome. Most *trattorie* worth their salt will make this themselves, in-house (*"fatto a casa"*), but always ask to be sure. There's nothing like fresh pasta! You often see this served with *amatriciana* or *alla gricia* (see below).

Tonnarelli

A thicker version of spaghetti, and another popular Roman pasta.

Pasta e ceci

Pasta with chickpeas. A very old and delicious recipe!

Pasta alla gricia

Another very simple, and old, Roman recipe, it's simply pasta (hopefully handmade!) with *pecorino*, black pepper, and *guanciale* (again, not really "bacon" and not *pancetta*, but pork jowl).

Pasta arrabbiata

Literally "angry" pasta, this is one for the spice-lovers. It's a pasta with a sauce of tomatoes, chopped garlic and a lot of *peperoncini* (red chili peppers)... hence the "angry"!

Cacio e pepe

One of the most classic Roman pastas, this is a pasta served with grated *pecorino* cheese, black pepper, and some of its own boiling water. It's simple, but decadent – like Rome's answer to macaroni and cheese.

Pasta alla carbonara

The second of Rome's most popular pastas, this is not like it's made back home. Although the sauce is creamy, there's no cream at all. Instead, the proper Roman *carbonara* is made of diced *guanciale*, eggs, and either parmesan or *pecorino*... and that's it.

Pasta all'amatriciana

Perhaps my favorite "comfort food" – and what I really crave when not in Rome – this is pasta in a sauce of *guanciale*, tomato, a little red pepper, a bit of wine, and *pecorino*. It's named after Amatrice, the Lazio town said to have come up with the dish. While the sauce might have a bit of garlic, most cooks frown on there being any onions.

Rigatoni con pajata

A pasta with *pajata*. *Pajata* is the intestine of an unweaned (read: milk-fed) lamb or calf. Those intestines are cleaned and skinned, but that partially-digested milk, called "chyme," is left inside. When cooked, it becomes thick and creamy. It's usually served in small tubes with a red sauce in pasta.

While all of that might sound disgusting – even some Romans shy away from trying it – it is, frankly, delicious.

This is one of Rome's many *cucina povera* dishes, food created from offal by people who couldn't afford anything else.

Saltimbocca alla romana

Veal wrapped in *prosciutto crudo* and sage, then rapidly fried. So tender and flavorful, the name literally means "jump-in-the-mouth" in Roman dialect.

Coda alla vaccinara

Oxtail, another member of the *cucina povera* clan, slow-cooked until it falls off the bone and usually served in a hearty tomato stew.

Involtini alla romana

Rolls of beef stuffed with carrots and celery and served in a tomato sauce.

Trippa

Tripe. Yes, that's stomach lining, often served simmered and finished with a tomato sauce. The texture is a bit like pasta, and if nobody tells you what you're eating, you might not even know.

Crostata di ricotta

A classic Roman dessert, this is a cheesecake made with ricotta. Just sweet enough, but nowhere near as cloying as many desserts elsewhere, it is often finished with chocolate or a fruit of the season.

A note on "Italian food"

Again, it's important to keep in mind that there really *is* no such thing as Italian food. Instead, there's Roman food, and Tuscan food, and Milanese food, and…

That being said, there also are some "Italian" foods that you could comb all of Italy for and still not find – except in the kinds of restaurants that dish up mediocre, microwaved food at inflated prices to tourists.

Why? Because these foods aren't Italian. They're Italian-American, Italian-British, or some other hybrid that was developed by immigrants after they left the home country. There's nothing wrong with this cuisine, and it's not "worse" than what you find in Italy (though some people will find they prefer the food in Italy, as it tends to be less greasy and fresher than its counterparts abroad). But if you try to look for these dishes in Italy, you'll usually be disappointed in one of two ways: Either you won't find a restaurant serving them, or you will but will have the kind of a terrible, overpriced meal that points to the fact that you've landed at a tourist trap.

Here are a few "Italian" dishes that you'll find much more easily in Chicago, New York or London than you will in Italy – and what to try instead.

1) Lobster fra' diavolo

This rich, spicy dish was likely served for the first time in the early 20th century – in New York. "I suspect that it came from Long Island," Italian-born cookbook author Anna Teresa Callen told the *New York Times* in the newspaper's intrepid attempt to track down the dish's origins. "A heavy tomato sauce with hot peppers, seafood, and pasta all in one dish is not Italian cooking," another Italian food writer said. Others pointed out that the dish hinges on using American lobsters, a tough find at even the most luxury of food establishments in contemporary Italy.

Instead, try: pasta all'arrabbiata

Pastas that incorporate seafood and tomatoes are common in southern Italy and Sicily, although rarely spicy and not heavy. If a spicy kick is what you're after, then while in Rome, look for *pasta all'arrabbiata*: "Angry pasta," which gets its name from using *peperoncini*, or red chile peppers, to give the otherwise-simple sauce (tomatoes, olive oil, and parsley) its kick.

2) Marinara sauce

This sauce wasn't even included in a book of Italian cooking compiled by the Accademia Italiana della Cucina in 2009. Somehow, though, it gained traction as a pop-culture reference to Italian(-American) culture in America by the 1930s.

Instead, try: pasta alla marinara... the Italian kind

In Naples and southern Italy, you can often order pasta with a "marinara" sauce – but this is a tomato sauce with shellfish, not the plain "tomato sauce" you might expect.

3) Spaghetti and meatballs

In his memoirs, a Sicilian named Niccolò de Quattrociocchi wrote that, while eating at an Italian restaurant in New York in the early 20th century, he encountered two "very fine, traditional American specialties" for the first time. One of these? Spaghetti and meatballs.

Instead, try: polpette al sugo

You can find meatballs in tomato sauce in Rome and south of Rome; they're just not served on pasta. They're often much smaller than those you'd see outside of Italy, particularly in the U.S. But there's a bonus: If you choose your *trattoria* carefully, they should also be much fresher. While frozen everything is starting to encroach on food culture in Italy, the trend is still a few years behind the U.S. In other words, it's the perfect place to try those meatballs without all that carbohydrate distraction.

4) Chicken or veal parmesan

Also not Italian. What *is* Italian, or at least southern Italian, is *melanzane alla parmigiana,* or what we know (roughly) as "eggplant parm" – eggplant fried and layered with tomato sauce, mozzarella, and parmesan, then baked. Using meat instead, and throwing it on top of pasta, was an invention of Italian immigrants in the United States and Canada.

The other Italian dish that Quattrociocchi was so tickled by?

Cotoletta parmigiana, or "veal parmesan". This one also seems to be an immigrant invention; at the very least, you don't see it at places that cater to Italians back in Italy. And, like putting chicken on pasta, the idea of layering melted cheese on meat is something that would make the noses of most of my Italian friends turn right up.

Instead, try: melanzane alla parmigiana

Similar concept, but with eggplant. Look for this in southern Italy, especially in Sicily (you can find it at some restaurants in Rome, too).

5) Garlic bread

Contrary to popular belief, you don't have to smell like a fresh garlic clove throughout your time in Italy. Italian dishes are much lighter on garlic than their Italian-American counterparts. (The same goes for onions). And in the country of olive oil, rubbing bread in butter is generally a strange thing to do, regardless. For that reason, it's thought that garlic bread was invented in the U.S. in the 1940s.

Instead, try: bruschetta al pomodoro

This bread is toasted, too – and even rubbed with a (slight! slight!) amount of garlic. It's then topped with lots of fresh tomatoes. Look for it in Rome, and remember two things: Not only can you get away with pronouncing it *broo-SKEHT-tah* here without sounding like a jerk (in fact, waiters who don't speak English might not know what you're ordering otherwise), but it's either an *antipasto* or a snack during *aperitivo* (a pre-dinner drink), not something to be served or consumed alongside a main course.

6) Fettuccine Alfredo

It's like macaroni and cheese ... with an Italian twist. Or so I always thought – until I moved to Italy. Turns out, there's only one restaurant I ever heard of that served it. The name? Alfredo's. It was created there in 1920 by the chef to appeal to American clientele. No surprise, really, since nothing about the dish appeals to traditional Italian palates; putting cream on pasta is so rarely done that, remember, even *pasta carbonara* uses no cream. And, again, there's the whole issue of using butter. But legend has it that, when honeymooning in Rome in 1920, Douglas Fairbanks and Mary Pickford liked Alfredo's pasta so much they brought the recipe back home. The gooey concoction has tortured American stomachs ever since.

Instead, try: cacio e pepe

This traditional Roman pasta is simply cheese and pepper, just like the name says. Pasta gets swirled with a mixture of Pecorino Romano cheese, fresh black pepper, and a touch of olive oil, a mixture melted together by the pasta's heat. And that's it. No fuss, no muss, no antacids needed.

7) Chicken on pasta, ever

"*Che schifo*," a friend of mine said when she first heard that this was a thing in the U.S. Her scorn needs no translation. Putting meatballs on pasta is something that Italians don't usually do, but still, like Quattrociocchi, can see the merit of (after all, many other pasta dishes incorporate meat into the sauce, like *ragu*). But that benefit of the doubt simply doesn't extend to chicken. It's a separate dish. End of story.

Instead, try: fish on pasta

This, for some reason, *is* okay (although, like meat in a *ragu*, it almost always will be broken up into small pieces, not served whole on top of a pile of pasta). Specialties vary across Italy's (sea- or river-proximate) regions, but some of the most delicious seafood pastas can be found in Sicily, where dishes incorporate local catches ranging from *pesce spada* (swordfish) to *sarde* (sardines).

8) Pasta primavera

Made with a mixture of pine nuts, tomatoes, string beans, frozen peas, and broccoli, this dish was invented by the wife of the owner of the New York restaurant Le Cirque. She tossed it together to feed a couple of guests during a trip to Canada. Le Cirque's owner, an Italian, actually refused to make it in the restaurant, saying it would "contaminate" the kitchen.

Instead, try:

This is such a strange dish, there's not really any kind of equivalent. But you could try *pasta broccoli e salsiccia* (pasta with broccoli and sausage), a southern Italian dish that'll get some of your greens in.

9) Penne alla vodka

Good luck getting to the bottom of this one. Like the other dishes on the list, in my way-too-many meals in Italy, I've never seen this; others say that it was a flash-in-the-pan trend (no pun intended) that hit Italy in the mid-1970s, then disappeared. In any case, vodka isn't, obviously, a traditionally Italian drink. And, again, a pasta sauce with cream – *penne alla vodka* usually includes tomatoes, onions, cream, and vodka – is pretty tough to find in the old country.

Instead, try: anything else

No, really. Anything else. Please. Penne alla vodka doesn't even make sense: What little flavor vodka has gets burned off in the cooking, leaving you with a sad tomato-onion-cream sauce. What did that vodka ever do to you? Instead, order any local specialty – anything – and if you really want to feel a little kick, follow up your dinner with an order of grappa or limoncello: Alcohol you'll actually be able to taste.

10) Cheesecake

It's the go-to dessert of Little Italy restaurants everywhere, but good luck finding this delicious, decadent dessert on menus in Italy… though some are starting to serve it in response to tourists asking.

Instead, try: cassata siciliana

Sweetened ricotta mixes are common in Southern Italy,

particularly in Naples and Sicily (although they're not generally as heavy, or sweet, as anything you'd taste in a cheesecake). They fill *cannoli, sfogliatelle,* and a myriad of other pastries. The closest to a cheesecake in terms of sheer decadence, though, is the *cassata siciliana,* a liquor-soaked sponge cake that gets layered with sweetened ricotta, covered in green almond paste, and iced; it likely took on its current appearance in the 18th century, when it would have been consumed only around Easter celebrations. In this case, in terms of richness, the Italian version might just give the Italian-American one a run for its money. It's not a Roman dish, but you can find it at Rome's various Sicilian bakeries, like I Dolci di Nonna Vicenza (near Campo dei Fiori) and Sicilia e Duci (Testaccio).

How to eat with dietary requirements

If you're a vegetarian or vegan – or have any other dietary restrictions – you might be wondering if it's possible to navigate Italy's restaurants, cafes, and grocery stores and still enjoy the food. Don't worry: It is.

For one, despite the stereotype, Italians are becoming more and more familiar with (and accepting of) lifestyles that exclude meat, dairy or something else. (Perhaps it makes sense that, as a culture especially concerned with the *benessere,* or well-being, that comes from daily life, they're more than understanding if you find that you just can't be your healthiest without making some dietary changes). In fact, even Berlusconi recently irritated the meat lobby by campaigning for a vegetarian Easter!

That being said, because those with such restrictions remain in the minority, it can be tough to find restaurants that will cater to you. Here are some tips.

Know that some ingredients, like butter and cream, you don't have to worry as much about

In restaurants in other countries, it's common to see dishes drenched in butter or cream sauces – not ideal if you're vegan or lactose-intolerant. But in Italy, the base for pretty much everything is olive oil. Some Italians don't even *own* butter. And heavy cream sauces, of the kind you have to be careful of in, say, France, are very rare.

Meanwhile, other traditions that crop up in Italian-American restaurants, like shaking grated cheese over every dish, you just don't see at restaurants in Italy. (Occasionally you'll be offered cheese to add to your pasta, but that's it).

That said, cream is a popular base for desserts, like *tiramisu* or *millefoglie*.

And avoiding meat is more difficult. *Guanciale* (pork jowl) is often used in tomato sauces for various pastas (although, if the menu describes each kind of pasta, *guanciale* should be listed), and *pancetta* often winds up in soups. *Fritti* also tend to have meat or fish inside, including even *fiori di zucca* and *suppli*. Always ask if you're unsure.

Lactose-intolerant? In Italy, you might be more tolerant than you think

If you consider yourself lactose-intolerant, you might find that you can eat dairy items in Italy that you can't handle back home. For one thing, some people find that it turns out that they're not intolerant of lactose – they just can't handle the preservatives and additives that tend to be added to dairy in the States, but aren't as much in Italy.

For another, when cheeses are aged, the bacteria actually consumes lactose. Most lactose, in fact, is gone after just three months of aging. On top of that, processed cheeses have more lactose than other cheeses. (Velveeta, for example, has 9.3 percent lactose). So you might find you're just fine when you eat Italy's harder, aged cheeses, like Parmigiano-Reggiano ("parmesan") or pecorino. (Even if you can't eat "parmesan cheese" in the States, of course, you might be able to in Italy: In the U.S., what's sold as "parmesan" is rarely the real thing).

For restricted diets, research restaurants in advance

For vegan or vegetarian restaurants, check out Happy Cow's list (happycow.net).

For gluten-free recommendations, try Puntarella Rossa (puntarellarossa.com) and the blog All Around is Gluten Free (allaroundisglutenfree.com). (You'll have to run both through Google Translate for English).

Have some fail-safe dishes in mind

For those with restricted diets, the good news is that Italian cities and regions tend to be known for particular dishes... and those dishes appear again and again on local menus. In Rome, for example, you'll see a lot of *amatriciana, cacio e pepe,* and *carbonara* (in fact, it's hard to find a Roman restaurant that doesn't offer these three dishes). And, while in other countries, each restaurant would probably make the dish almost completely differently from the next, that's not so much the trend in Italy, where at traditional trattorias, people like to know *exactly* what they're getting when they order a certain dish (and where they want it to taste exactly like Grandma's!). As a result, it helps to familiarize yourself with local specialties you can eat ahead of time. More on some safe bets for different diets later.

Be specific about what you don't eat

Rather than assume a server understands what you mean by vegan, pescatarian or vegetarian, go easy on the poor waiter and be specific. After you've picked out a couple of things that might be okay, ask: "*È senza glutine?*" (Is it gluten-free?), "*È senza carne?*" (It's without meat?), "*È senza formaggio?*" (It's without cheese?) or "*È senza noci?*" (It's without nuts?).

Describe what you don't eat as an intolerance or as something you don't digest

It's true that, while things have changed, not every Italian (especially those serving at a traditional trattoria) understand cutting out pasta, cheese or something else as a lifestyle choice. What they *do* understand is digestion (as the number of yogurts, drinks, and other foods marketed as being "good for digestion" attests!). So consider saying *"Non posso digerire..."* (I can't digest ...) instead of "I'm gluten-free", for example.

If you're a vegan or vegetarian, then order...

bruschetta: A traditional *antipasto,* this is toasted bread rubbed with oil, garlic, and with a variety of toppings to choose from. *Bruschetta al pomodoro* is bruschetta with tomato, and we've yet to see it with any meat thrown in!

pasta all'arrabbiata: Literally "angry pasta," this is pasta with a spicy tomato sauce. There shouldn't be any meat or cheese (generally, if cheese isn't already tossed with the pasta, as in *cacio e pepe,* it won't be sprinkled on after – you may be offered it, but can of course say no).

pizza: If you're vegan or lactose-intolerant, opt for the *pizza marinara,* which is pizza with tomato sauce (no cheese). If you're vegetarian, you have lots of options, the most simple of them the classic *pizza margherita* (tomato sauce and mozzarella). If meat's not listed as a topping, it won't be on the pizza. Just make sure you understand what all of the toppings are! *Peperoni,* by the way, isn't "pepperoni", but peppers.

grilled vegetables in the *contorni* section: *Contorni* means "sides," and this is usually where you'll find a plethora of vegetable dishes, from grilled eggplant to roasted potatoes to boiled spinach (depending on the season).

If you are gluten-free...

polenta: A dish made from boiled cornmeal, *polenta* is particularly popular in northern Italy. It's tougher to find in Rome, but keep your eye out.

risotto: A rice-based dish that's especially popular in Milan, Venice, and the north. The broth might have gluten, so ask. Again, this is a tougher find at a traditional trattoria in Rome, but if you're at a place that's a little more "contemporary" or fusion Italian cuisine, they may have it.

gnocchi: How *gnocchi* is made can vary, so make sure you ask how it's made. One traditional way to make it is with potato, in which case you're good to go; sometimes, though, flour is used. Just ask. Gnocchi is common at traditional Roman restaurants.

grilled vegetables in the *contorni* section: Again, *contorni* means "sides," and this is usually where you'll find a plethora of vegetable dishes, from grilled eggplant to roasted potatoes to boiled spinach (depending on the season).

Eating in season

When in Rome, do as the Romans (traditionally) do: Eat ingredients that are in season.

Although everyone wants to try a Roman artichoke when they're in Rome, *carciofi romaneschi* are only in season from February to May. If you see artichokes on a menu at any other time of year, they're not Roman, so they won't be a real taste of the famous dish (they'll either be from somewhere else in Italy or imported from abroad, depending on the month).

Even worse, creating demand for out-of-season produce throws everything out of whack, from hurting local farmers who are growing in-season foods to damaging the environment by increasing high-mileage imports... the definition of invasive tourism.

To help you know what's in season when in Italy, here's a quick list of general guidelines:

January

In season: beets (*bietole*), broccoli (*broccoli*), cabbage (*cavoli*), cauliflower (*cavolfiori*), chicory (*cicoria*), oranges (*arance*), puntarelle (*puntarelle*), spinach (*spinaci*)

February

In season: Roman artichokes (*carciofi romaneschi*), broccoli (*broccoli*), cabbage (*cavoli*), cauliflower (*cavolfiori*), chicory (*cicoria*), oranges (*arance*), puntarelle (*puntarelle*), spinach (*spinaci*)

March

In season: Roman artichokes (*carciofi romaneschi*), asparagus (*asparagi*), broccoli (*broccoli*), cabbage (*cavoli*), cauliflower (*cavolfiori*), chicory (*cicoria*), oranges (*arance*), spinach (*spinaci*)

April

In season: Roman artichokes (*carciofi romaneschi*), asparagus (*asparagi*), beets (*bietole*), cabbage (*cavoli*), carrots (*carote*), cauliflower (*cavolfiori*), chicory (*cicoria*), oranges (*arance*), peas (*piselli*), strawberries (*fragole*)

May

In season: Roman artichokes (*carciofi romaneschi*), asparagus (*asparagi*), beets (*bietole*), carrots (*carote*), cherries (*ciliegie*), chicory (*cicoria*), fava beans (*fave*), green beans (*fagiolini*), onions (*cipolle*), oranges (*arance*), peas (*piselli*), strawberries (*fragole*)

June

In season: apricots (*albicocche*), asparagus (*asparagi*), beets (*bietole*), cherries (*ciliegie*), chicory (*cicoria*), cucumber (*cetrioli*), fava beans (*fave*), green beans (*fagiolini*), melon (*meloni*), onions (*cipolle*), peaches (*pesche*), peas (*piselli*), strawberries (*fragole*), tomatoes (*pomodori*), zucchini (*zucchine*), zucchini flowers (*fiori di zucca*)

July

In season: apricots (*albicocche*), beans (*fagioli*), beets (*bietole*), cherries (*ciliegie*), chicory (*cicoria*), cucumber (*cetrioli*), eggplant (*melanzane*), fava beans (*fave*), figs (*fichi*), green beans (*fagiolini*), melon (*meloni*), onions (*cipolle*), peaches (*pesche*), peas (*piselli*), peppers (*peperoni*), strawberries (*fragole*), tomatoes (*pomodori*), watermelon (*angurie*), zucchini (*zucchine*), zucchini flowers (*fiori di zucca*)

August

In season: apricots (*albicocche*), beans (*fagioli*), beets (*bietole*), carrots (*carote*), cherries (*ciliegie*), chicory (*cicoria*), cucumber (*cetrioli*), eggplant (*melanzane*), figs (*fichi*), green beans (*fagiolini*), melon (*meloni*), onions (*cipolle*), peaches (*pesche*), pears (*pere*), peppers (*peperoni*), potatoes (*patate*), strawberries (*fragole*), tomatoes (*pomodori*), watermelon (*angurie*), zucchini (*zucchine*), zucchini flowers (*fiori di zucca*)

September
In season: apples (*mele*), beets (*bietole*), broccoli (*broccoli*), carrots (*carote*), chicory (*cicoria*), cucumber (*cetrioli*), eggplant (*melanzane*), figs (*fichi*), grapes (*uva*), peaches (*pesche*), pears (*pere*), peppers (*peperoni*), potatoes (*patate*), pumpkin (*zucca*), tomatoes (*pomodori*), zucchini (*zucchine*)

October
In season: apples (*mele*), beets (*bietole*), broccoli (*broccoli*), cabbage (*cavoli*), carrots (*carote*), cauliflower (*cavolfiori*), chestnuts (*castagne*), chicory (*cicoria*), eggplant (*melanzane*), grapes (*uva*), pears (*pere*), potatoes (*patate*), pumpkin (*zucca*)

November
In season: beets (*bietole*), broccoli (*broccoli*), cabbage (*cavoli*), carrots (*carote*), cauliflower (*cavolfiori*), chestnuts (*castagne*), chicory (*cicoria*), eggplant (*melanzane*), grapes (*uva*), oranges (*arance*), pumpkin (*zucca*), puntarelle (*puntarelle*), spinach (*spinaci*)

December
In season: beets (*bietole*), broccoli (*broccoli*), cabbage (*cavoli*), cauliflower (*cavolfiori*), chicory (*cicoria*), oranges (*arance*), puntarelle (*puntarelle*), spinach (*spinaci*)

Ten etiquette mistakes not to make eating in Italy

When it comes to food, Italians love etiquette. It doesn't matter if you're at a fine-dining establishment with jacketed waiters or chowing down on pizza at a plastic table: There are some things that will tend to get you dirty looks. Here are 10 ways to make servers into enemies and annoy neighboring Italians!

1) Expecting (American-style) breakfast

Unless your hotel provides it, don't expect your first meal of the day to be anything like back home. Most Italians start their day with something light, like a coffee and *cornetto* or perhaps cereal. The idea of starting your day with a big fry-up, or even just good old scrambled eggs and pancakes, is a completely foreign concept.

If you have to have the full spread in the morning, either pick a hotel that explicitly offers American-style brunch or plan to grocery shop and cook your own food.

2) Ordering coffee before or with a meal

What horror! Coffee is seen as a way to help you digest your meal, so drinking it alongside is seen as misguided, even dangerous. (Really!). If you must have a caffeine hit before a meal (and really, when you're facing a 3-hour dinner that starts at 9pm, who can blame you), duck around the corner for a quick espresso at a nearby café.

And yes, an espresso, because another deadly sin is:

3) Having a *cappuccino* after noon

With all of its foamy milk, cappuccino, or any coffee drink that includes a lot of milk, is seen as a breakfast drink. So when the clock strikes noon, Romans usually change their order to espresso or *lungo* – never *cappuccino*.

4) Asking for olive oil, or olive oil and vinegar, to dip your bread into

In general, you only see Italians dipping bread, alone, into olive oil when they're doing an olive oil tasting. At meals, it's just not done. Bread instead is seen as an accompaniment to your *primi* and *secondi*, not as a way to fill you up pre-dinner.

5) Requesting parmesan for your pizza

It doesn't even matter if you know the proper word for it

("*parmigiano*"). Putting it on pizza is seen as a sin, like putting Jell-O on a fine chocolate mousse. When a visiting friend of mine did this recently at a pizzeria in Rome, the waiter's response was uncompromising: "*Parmigiano per la pizza?*" he asked disdainfully. And this was a pizzeria that's *used* to tourists. Imagine how they'd treat you at a pizzeria that wasn't.

6) In fact, putting parmesan on anything with which it isn't explicitly offered

Remember that many pasta dishes in Italy aren't meant for parmesan. In Rome, for example, the traditional cheese is *pecorino,*and that's what usually goes on classics like *pasta carbonara* and *amatriciana*. Not parmesan. As a rule of thumb: If they don't offer it to you, don't ask for it.

7) Asking the *server* for more water, wine, or food

The person who brings your food isn't (usually) the same person who takes your order. You might get a dirty look if you put an order in with the server, or, at least, find your order ignored.

8) Ordering *acqua del rubinetto* (tap water) at anything but a café or bar

Yes, Rome's water is perfectly safe. But when eating out, Italians always drink bottled water. (Most restaurants have the option of a big bottle of water for the table to share, rather than the small, individual bottles you find at the cafés). I've been told that this is because there's a lot of calcium in the tap water, so Italians mix it up with bottled so they don't get kidney stones. I've also been told it's because Italians simply don't trust anything provided by the state.

Who knows. But it's what the locals do, and restaurants will simply refuse you if you ask for tap water (although bars and cafés, when selling you a cocktail or a coffee, should allow it).

Bonus: To really look local, ask for sparkling ("*frizzante*", "*con gas*" or, for the slightly-sparkling version, "*leggermente gassata*") instead of still ("*naturale*").

9) Eating on the go

Like the Parisians, Romans look down on anyone chowing down on bus, metro, or on foot. It's anathema to the entire philosophy of eating: Meals should be enjoyed sitting down – over at least an hour. Eating while doing anything else is seen as sloppy, desperate (can you really be that hungry?), and missing the whole point.

The one exception: Gelato, which you'll see whole families tucking into on their Sunday evening strolls.

10) Getting annoyed that your bill hasn't yet come

It hasn't come because… you must ask for it. In Italy, it's seen as rude for a waiter to bring your bill and whisk away your plates as soon as you've finished your food. Instead, you're supposed to have the liberty (and luxury) of lingering at your table, finishing your wine, and even ordering a coffee.

Once you're ready to go, just signal for the waiter and say, *"Il conto, per favore."* (When he visited, my grandfather remembered this phrase, and how to pronounce it, with a series of pictures: eel cone toe, pear fahvore… okay, so the *favore* didn't work quite so well). Too complicated? The universal squiggly-finger-in-the-air hand signal will always work, too.

Of course, as a caveat, it's not as if I always adhere to Italian etiquette. Or that all Italians always do. And yes, as a tourist, you'll be forgiven more than most. These are just some guidelines that can help you, well, not embarrass yourself. If you choose to follow them.

If you don't, just remember… You have been warned!

Ordering coffee in Rome

A traveler to Rome once told me a story about her first time ordering coffee in Italy. She knew the "Italian" lingo of coffee from Starbucks, so she thought she was all set when she arrived in Italy and, at her first café stop, proudly ordered a *"latte"*.

The server looked at her funny. *"Latte? Caldo o freddo?"* (Hot or cold?).

She spoke a little Italian, so it was her turn to look at *him* funny: *"Caldo,* of course!" she said.

The server disappeared for a moment, returned, and handed her exactly what she'd asked for – a cup of hot milk.

Another time, I was interviewing the owner of Caffè Sant'Eustachio, widely considered to be the best café in Rome, and I asked him why he thought not a single Starbucks had opened in Rome. He scoffed. *"Macchiatto, espresso, cappuccino,"* he said. "These are all *Italian* names. Why would we buy the American version of these drinks when we're the ones who *invented* them?"

Good point.

So, suffice it to say: Italian coffee culture is a big deal. And coffee here *isn't* like coffee in the United States, or anywhere else. You could write a whole book on coffee in Italy. (In fact, people have!).

But if you just want the basics to get you through, here are some things to know.

A "bar" is really a "café"

The number of places labeled "bar" in your average Italian city would make you think all Italians have a drinking problem. If they do, it is, of course, a coffee drinking problem. That's because a "bar" is actually what Americans would call a "café." (In Italian, it's spelled *caffè*).

To make things more confusing, *caffè* actually means not only the coffee establishment, but also a "coffee" itself.

Most Italians drink coffee standing at the bar

Unless you *really* need to rest those feet, make like an Italian and order, and drink, your coffee at the bar. It's often half or a third the price of sitting at a table, especially near a tourist site. And it's where the locals tend to hang out.

At the bar, you usually have to pay for your coffee *before* ordering it

Not every café actually enforces this rule. But as a rule of thumb, it's better to go to the cash register first and say what you're going to get – "*due caffè,*" "*un cornetto,*" etc. – and pay first.

Take the receipt you're given and don't throw it out. Instead, bring it to the bar with you, and hand it to the server, to get served.

Don't order a cappuccino after noon

I mentioned this in the previous section. But it's worth mentioning again. Especially at local cafés that aren't used to tourists, if you order a cappuccino in the afternoon or evening, you might get a *very* funny look.

Know what coffee is what

Obviously, a *latte* in an American or British Starbucks isn't the same as a *latte* in Italy. (Since the word is Italian and does mean "milk," of course, Italians might have the edge on saying that the Starbucks version is plain old wrong).

Instead, here are the most popular Italian coffee phrases you should know:

• *Caffè:* This literally means "coffee," but folks – in Italy, it's an espresso! You don't have to say "espresso" when you order (although if they know you're a tourist, they might ask just to make sure). I once saw a whole family react with shock when the "*caffè*" they ordered came… as espresso, rather than filtered coffee. Oops!

• *Cappuccino:* Espresso topped up with hot, foamed milk. It's named after the *Cappuccini,* or Capuchin monks, because of the color of their hoods.

• *Caffè macchiato:* This means a "spotted" or "stained" coffee, and in this case, it's spotted with a splash of hot milk.

• *Latte macchiato:* Guess what this means? "Spotted milk" – in this case, a lot of milk with a spot of coffee.

• *Caffè americano:* American-style filter coffee doesn't (usually) exist here. Instead, if you order an "American coffee," you'll get

Italy's best approximate: espresso with hot water added.

• *Caffè lungo:* A "long" coffee, i.e. with more water. It's different than an *americano* because the difference actually happens at the espresso machine: When the espresso is actually being pulled, the process is slowed down so there's twice as much water involved.

Help yourself to the *cremina*

Except for icy, summery drinks like *caffè shakerato* (coffee "shaken up" with ice and sugar), coffee doesn't usually come with any sugar in it. Instead, it's up to you to add sugar, usually found in either jars or packets there on the counter. Some places also will have tubs of *cremina*, which is foam whipped with sugar. If you want to (and you aren't grossed out by the communal tub), you can spoon some right into your coffee to give it a sweet little kick.

Hello, gelato!

If you're like many travelers to Italy, one of the foods you might be most excited to try is gelato.

First, let's clear up one misconception. Gelato is *not* just the "Italian version" of ice cream.

Gelato versus ice cream: the smack-down

I love ice cream as much as the next girl. But when it comes to my choice for frozen sustenance, I'd go gelato all the way.

Here are three reasons why.

1) Less butterfat –> melt-in-your-mouth texture

In properly-made gelato, just 4 to 8 percent of the mix is made up by butterfat. Compare that to an average of 14 percent for ice cream in the United States.

The result? It's not just that gelato is less "fatty" than ice cream. It's also that gelato freezes less solidly than ice cream (and is actually served about 10 to 15 degrees warmer). So it melts in your mouth faster. (It also melts in your cup faster. I recently saw a review on Tripadvisor for a gelateria, complaining the gelato wasn't as "firm" as it should be and melted too quickly. That's actually a good sign, not a bad one).

2) Higher density -> more flavor

Gelato also has a much higher density than ice cream. To make ice cream, producers mix cream, milk, and sugar – and then add air, which increases volume, and water, which increases weight. But all that air and water, of course, cuts down on the flavor.

In Europe, however, regulations prevent foodmakers from using that kind of process, called "overrun". In Italy, in fact, you can't legally increase an ice cream's weight with water and volume with air. Hence, more flavor.

3) Not made for long-term storage -> fresher

Finally, most commercial ice creams elsewhere are made for long-term storage. In fact, that's why they're both more fully frozen and have a higher fat content.

Gelato, though, is frozen quickly in small batches. So it's much fresher. Truly artisanal gelato, in fact, has to be eaten within a couple of days of being made.

So when it comes to gelato versus ice cream, I'd pick gelato every time. But not all gelato is made equally. Want to try the *best* of the yummy stuff? Read on.

How to sniff out Rome's best gelaterias

Here's the thing: The above details aside, not every gelato you have in Italy will be perfect... or even that fresh. Europe's stricter food regulations aside, one thing in Italy you *can* do, for example, is buy an industrial "mix", add flavorings, put it in stainless steel trays, and call the gelato "artisanal".

That's why you can't trust just any old gelateria that uses the words artisanal (or *"artigianale"*). Many of the gelaterias in Rome, and throughout Italy, use lots of chemicals, artificial flavorings, and thickeners.

How do you pick the real artisanal *gelaterie* for the best, freshest gelato? Here are two top tips to keep in mind.

1) Run from pretty, puffy clouds of gelato

Ever seen pictures of a gelateria showing tub after tub of fluffy, perfectly-formed gelato, each kind usually topped with fruit, or cookies, or some other over-the-top decoration? It looks like some kind of gelato fantasy, right?

Well, it's not a fantasy. It's real, and you see it across Italy. But that's pretty much the only real thing about it.

The fluffiness comes from thickeners (bad!). And having enough of each flavor to make such a big, puffy pile means that the gelato isn't fresh, but made in advance and reused each day (also bad!).

Finally, I don't know why, but the whole tradition of decorating the gelato with fruit and so on just isn't something I've ever seen at a proper, artisanal gelateria. Maybe the decorations are a distraction device?

2) If the colors are too bright, the gelato ain't right

If it's made without chemicals, a gelato's colors, regardless of the flavor, will be muted. Mint will be white; so will apple. Pistachio will be a very light, beigey green. Banana will be beige. *Nothing* will be bright.

So when you enter a gelateria, scan the colors in front of you. Do any of them look closer to a Crayola crayon than to, I don't know, what an actual fruit would look like mashed up in a blender? Then turn around and find a place where you can try the good stuff.

After all, you're only here for a limited time. There's no reason to waste a single bite! (And if you want recommendations for my favorite artisanal gelaterias in Rome, read on).

What to know about tipping

As you may have read elsewhere, Italians don't have a tipping culture the same way some other countries do. Most locals will round up on a bill by leaving a few coins on the table, but that still means leaving far less than some other nationalities, particularly Americans, tend to do (think leaving €50 for a €47 bill).

While I know it makes some travelers uncomfortable, I strongly believe that visitors to Italy should do the same. For one thing, waiting tables in Italy is much different than waiting tables in the States. Many Italian waiters are paid off the books, meaning they're not paying taxes. And if they are on the books, then they get paid vacations (some six weeks per year or more), paid sick leave, and, of course, national healthcare. Not to mention that many waiters are actually the family members of the owner, and may even live at home, so in theory, the overall profits of the restaurant may be more or less shared.

Regardless, by leaving 20% tips, tourists gradually change the system so that servers come to expect that much, and other consequences could follow – such as servers' wages being decreased.

So what should you do? If *servizio* has been added to your bill, then leave nothing on top. If it hasn't, then, of course, it's up to you, but I'd urge you to consider leaving just a few coins.

As mentioned previously, note that sometimes, a waiter might make the point of dropping a bill off to a table of tourists and, if *servizio* isn't on the bill, saying, "Service is not included." No, this is not his helpful way of clueing you in – because he would never say that to a table of Italians. Instead, he's learned that those magic words get English speakers, especially Americans, to take out their wallets and leave an extra 20 percent… without realizing they don't have to (and possibly shouldn't).

How not to get ripped off eating in Rome

Getting ripped off isn't something that will necessarily happen to you when you eat out in Rome. And if you follow my suggestions for where to eat, it probably won't happen at all.

That said, it's not uncommon. And when it happens, it's a bummer.

Many tourists think that it's just part of the deal when it comes to traveling in another country. But it doesn't have to be. Here are some tips.

The farther away from a tourist site you eat, the less likely you are to be ripped off

In Rome, high-risk areas include Rome's Piazza Navona, Trevi Fountain, Spanish Steps, Piazza del Popolo, and the Colosseum. In general, whenever you see as many non-Italians as Italians, be on your guard.

Other tip-offs that you're in a touristy establishment: There's a "host" outside the door asking you to come in (any Italian restaurant catering to locals, not tourists, won't have this, since they'll be jam-packed with diners no matter what), there's a menu with pictures, or there's a big sign that says "Tourist Menu" or even "No service!" or "No cover charge!". (More on that later).

That said? If you really want to avoid getting ripped off, the sad truth is that you have to have your wits about you no matter where you're eating.

If you sit down in an Italian café, know the price differences

Unless your feet are just killing you, avoid sitting down in the kind of place that Italians call a "bar" and we call a "café." As soon as you sit down, the price of whatever you're eating doubles or triples, which is why you see Italians usually taking their coffee and *cornetti* standing up. Even if a server at the café suggested you sit, the price will, most likely, still be higher.

If you do decide to sit down, then always walk in and check out the prices above the counter. (These prices are almost always inside, above the bar). Usually there is one column for "Banco" and one for "Tavolo". "Banco" is the price if you stand at the bar; "Tavolo" is if you're sitting.

When you ask for the bill, if you want to be super careful, you can ask for it to be itemized. (Say *"il conto dettagliato"* ["eel cone-toe deh-tahl-yah-toe] or *""il conto lungo"* ["eel cone-toe loon-go"]). This minimizes the chance that someone will simply come up with a random price to charge you. If any of the items on the bill aren't what you ordered, or if the prices are different than what you saw on the price list inside, ask why. You know what the prices for the various items were supposed to be *al tavolo*, because they've been posted and, legally, that's what they have to be. Don't let the waiter talk you into anything different.

At restaurants, know what you do and don't have to pay for

Yes, you do have to pay for water. (You can ask for *"acqua dal rubinetto,"* tap water, but it's often seen as a bit rude. Plus, those glasses of tap water will take ages to get refilled by your waiter, if they're refilled at all!). At moderately-priced places, a large bottle of mineral water for the table should cost no more than €2.

Yes, you do also have to pay for bread. This is the *"pane e coperto"* charge; more on that in a moment.

Yes, you do have to pay for that antipasto or *focaccia*. Even if the way the waiter asked you if you wanted it made it sound like it would be free. ("Would you like just a little bit of focaccia while you decide?").

And yes, you have to pay for that *digestivo* of limoncello or amaro or grappa... sometimes. Here's how to tell: If the waiter asks you if you want an after-dinner drink after you've eaten but *before* he's brought the bill, you'll probably be charged. If he asks you if you want one *after* he's brought the bill and/or you've paid, it's probably a little "thank you" on the house. Needless to say, unless you're a regular at a restaurant, the latter is the rarer situation.

Avoid giving the waiter the power over what, or how much, to bring

Sometimes, waiters will ask if you would like an *antipasto* for the table. Most of the time, this is fine! Occasionally, though, the *antipasto* winds up costing an arm and a leg – and you don't realize it until you get the bill.

So instead of telling the waiter to just bring you something, order specifically from the menu, with the quantity you'd like, and be clear. "*Vorrei un'antipasto per due,*" you could say (an antipasto for two), even if there are four of you. That's fine.

The other item to watch is fish. Since fish is usually charged by weight at restaurants, this can get a little confusing. You say you want the fish of the day that's around a certain weight, the waiter brings out a lovely, fresh-caught one to show you that's "around" that weight, and then miraculously, when the bill comes, it turns out that fish was a little heavier than you expected. Unfortunately, there's not a lot you can do about this, other than to double-check the weight a few times with the waiter before you agree to have them cook it.

Getting the bill at a restaurant

When your waiter brings you a bill (remember, you have to ask for it!), make sure that it's itemized. (Again, ask for "*il conto dettagliato*" or "*il conto lungo*"). Sometimes, restaurants will just write a total number down, or even just say it. In that case, ask for the itemized bill. It's the only way to know if you're being charged what you should be – and it just happens to be the only bill that's legal. More on that in a bit!

What's that "*pane e coperto*" charge?

When an Italian restaurant charges you for bread, it's generally not per basket. Instead, the price is per head, and in Rome, typically about €1 or €1.50 per person, up to €2 at a fairly touristy or expensive place.

The caveat with "*pane e coperto*", though, is that *this charge should be written on the menu*. Maybe it's in small letters, maybe it's on the back page, but it should be there.

If it's not? Say something and the charge should be removed.

What about a charge for "*servizio*"?

If an item has been added, probably 10 but up to 20 percent, called "*servizio*", that's "service."

Honestly, you shouldn't really be seeing this on your bill in Rome. It tends to be done only at fairly touristic places (which you're avoiding, right?).

If it is added, though, just make sure it was written on the menu. Again, it *can't* be added to your bill if it wasn't written on the menu. Finally, if you're charged *servizio*, *do not* add a tip on top. That *is* the tip. Countless Americans wind up being double-charged because they don't realize this.

Also, note that some restaurants try to attract tourists by having a sign saying "No service charge!". That's fine... but it means the place is pretty touristy. (A place that catered to Italians in Rome wouldn't have *servizio* anyway, so a local spot wouldn't make a big deal about not having it, especially not in English). And so, somewhat counterintuitively, a sign proclaiming no *servizio* isn't necessarily a good thing, either.

Think you've been ripped off anyway and want to take action?

When presented with a confusing or ridiculous bill, 90 percent of people won't do anything about it. They'll pay and leave. But for the rest of the day, they'll be seething. And it does a disservice to future tourists, since the restaurants learn that foreigners won't speak up.

So remember: You *do* have control in this situation. Here's what you do.

First, simply point out the discrepancy to the waiter and ask, politely but firmly, for it to be fixed. This is why you got that itemized bill. Even if he doesn't speak much English, you can point to the specific item. For *servizio* or *pane e coperto,*the most useful phrase is often "*Non è scritto sul menu*" (this was not written on the menu: "Nohn ay skree-toe sool meh-noo"). Often, that's all that's needed.

If he argues with you, show that you know what you're talking about (you saw the "banco" versus "tavolo" prices so you *know* what a cappuccino costs sitting down, etc.). He still won't back down? You don't have to give up. Here's where you pull out all the stops.

If you've been ripped off and they won't fix it, you could always bring out the big guns

Your polite requests haven't done anything to remove that 20 percent *servizio* that was added to your bill unannounced, or to get the proper *tavolo* price for your cafe meal instead of tacking on €20 more? You still have power. In fact, a lot of power.

This is what restaurants, cafes and bars in Italy really, really, *really* don't want you to know: A vast majority of the time, the receipt they're issuing you is not a real receipt. That means they're not paying taxes on the meal you just had. It's off the books. And that's illegal.

Often, by the way, what many visitors assume is the "real" receipt but isn't is the *preconto*.

Here's what happens: The waiter brings you something that looks to *you* like a receipt, so you leave the cash and walk away. What you don't realize is that the waiter is the one who's supposed to take that first "receipt" *and* the cash, then bring back change and the *proper* (fiscal!) receipt. Some of what you see above were the *"preconti"*… but, even after bringing back change, the waiter never brought back the proper *conto*.

How does all of this give *you* the power? Because, if an establishment has taken advantage of you, it's more than likely that you're holding one of these illegal receipts in your hand. And in that case, here's what you do.

Show them the receipt… and say the following three words: *"Guardia di finanza"*. ["Gwahr-dee-yah dee feeh-nahn-zah."]

These three words are enough to scare any Italian business-owner. Why? The *guardia* is like Italy's I.R.S. … with guns. They mean business. And they can do everything from levy huge fines to shut businesses down.

It's a pretty last-case scenario. But with those three magic words, your bill should be fixed… quickly.

My top spots for food

If you're relying on a guidebook or any information more than a couple of years old for restaurant recommendations, be ware: The quality of restaurants changes *quickly* here in Rome. A place that was fantastic yesterday gets a little recognition, a few write-ups, and boom, it goes downhill.

So checking up on a restaurant's reputation online can help. Not on Tripadvisor, though. While I recommend looking at Tripadvisor for reviews of, say, tour companies, I really, really don't recommend it for restaurant recommendations. Most of the top 20 places recommended are atrocious, and I can only assume it's because some spots have learned how to game the system, or because Tripadvisor members confuse getting a glass of free limoncello for an excellent, authentic Roman meal. It's unclear.

Instead, check out local food blogs like that by Katie Parla (p a r l a f o o d . c o m) and E l i z a b e t h M i n c h i l l i (elizabethminchilliinrome.com) and Italian food sites like Gambero Rosso (gamberorosso.it).

All that said? Here are some of *my* current favorites, including restaurants, wine bars, gelato shops and food markets. Just remember to check their website, or call, to make sure they're open the day you want to go – and, for many the restaurants, it's worth booking in advance.

Restaurants and cafés

Alle Carrette (Monti, near the Forum)
This is a neighborhood pizzeria at its best, with cozy but no-frills decor, lots of locals and, most importantly, crisp, thin-crust Roman pizza straight out of the wood oven. The *fritti* (fried foods, like zucchini flowers) are good, too. Telephone: +39 066792770. Address: Via Madonna dei Monti 95.

Armando al Pantheon (Pantheon)
Since 1961, Armando's has been serving up traditional, Roman

dishes right next to the Pantheon–and he's been making it in the guidebooks, too. The constant mentions of Armando's make it all the more surprising that both the food, and prices, remain good. Look for *pasta e ceci* (pasta with chickpeas) on Fridays, and don't miss the damn-good *torta antica Roma* to finish everything off. Reservations highly recommended. Telephone: +39 06 68803034. Address: Salita de' Crescenzi 31. *armandoalpantheon.it*

Cesare al Casaletto (Monteverde)

Here's why Cesare al Casaletto is great: Most trattorias in Rome, including every place mentioned above, flub *some*thing. Often, it's the meat courses. Sometimes, it's the service. But not Cesare. From start to finish, you can expect a top-notch Roman meal. At a good price. With friendly (!) servers. Which is why this place is massively popular – with locals, and also, increasingly, with tourists. That says a lot, particularly since, located at the very last stop on the number 8 tram, it's well off the beaten path. It couldn't be simpler to get to; you can get on the tram at Piazza Venezia, and riding it to the end takes about 25 minutes. Still, for many people, the idea of going "all the way" out to Monteverde while on a vacation in Rome is a little bit of a mental block. It's one that I'd recommend getting past. Reservations highly recommended. Telephone: +39 06536015. Address: Via del Casaletto 45.

Da Bucatino (Testaccio)

Da Bucatino is the quintessential Roman trattoria, down to the hit-or-miss service, reliably solid (if not life-changing) dishes, help-yourself *antipasti* bar and no-frills, casual atmosphere. And don't get me started on how much better it is than its (inexplicably) more famous neighbor, Da Felice. Telephone: +39 065746886 Address: Via Luca della Robbia 84/86.

Da Teo (Trastevere)

While hard-core *trasteverini* will swear up and down that the heart of Trastevere has the best food in Rome, don't believe them; thanks to the quarter's newfound popularity, mediocre meals are more and more commonplace. But not, luckily, at Da Teo. Grab an outdoor table, if you can, to enjoy the lovely and all-but-impossible-to-find tiny Piazza del Ponziani, and order one of the many traditional Roman plates on the menu. My two favorites: the *cacio e pepe* and *alla gricia* pastas. Reservations highly recommended. Telephone: +39 06 581 8355. Address: Piazza del Ponziani 7. *trattoriadateo.it*

Fa-bio (Prati, near the Vatican museums)

Looking for lunch on the go near the Vatican... that uses fresh, organic ingredients? This is your stop! Fa-bio, located just a 2-minutes' walk from the Vatican museum entrance and exit, is a tiny hole-in-the-wall dishing up made-to-order salads, sandwiches, soups, and smoothies – from all organic ingredients. Telephone: +39 0664525810. Address: Via Germanico 43.

Flavio al Velavevodetto (Testaccio and Trastevere)

Slow Food founder Carlo Petrini is a fan of this restaurant, which now has locations in both Trastevere and Testaccio – and so am I. The traditional Roman dishes are delicious, the servers on-point, and the ambience lovely (choose between an outdoor terrace or an indoor spot overlooking the ancient Roman jars that make up Monte Testaccio). Reservations highly recommended. Telephone: +39 065744194. Address: Via Monte Testaccio 97. *flavioalvelavevodetto.it*

Hostaria Romana (Piazza Barberini)

Hostaria Romana is old-school. The tables are crammed together, past diners have scrawled their signatures on the wall, and if two people at your table order the same pasta, it's spooned out of a pan right at your table. Fortunately, the dishes are old-school, too. Nothing here is going to blow your mind with creativity, but that's not the purpose of, say, a like-your-*nonna-romana*-made-it *amatriciana*: We're talking simple ingredients done well. Telephone: +39 064745284. Address: Via Boccaccio 1. *hostariaromana.it*

La Gatta Mangiona (Monteverde)

This "Slow Food" pizzeria is a little out of the way, but so worth it… especially if you prefer thick-crust pizza to the traditional Roman thin-crust. Pizzas range from the classic to the creative, always with top-notch, in-season ingredients, and the artisanal beer list is great, too. Telephone: +39 065346702. Address: Via F. Ozanam 30. *lagattamangiona.com*

La Matricianella (Piazza Navona)

With its dark wood panelling (and handful of outdoor tables), book-sized wine list and very good traditional Roman dishes, this is always one of my top spots to eat in the center of Rome – which can be a tough place to find a good, and good-value, meal. Reservations highly recommended. Telephone: +39 066832100. Address: Via del Leone 4. *matricianella.it*

L'Asino d'Oro (Monti, near the Forum)

Here's where to go when you want something different from *cucina romana* – even creative *cucina romana*. The food here is Umbrian, with a contemporary twist. Look for deliciousness like stewed wild boar in a sweet wine sauce. The atmosphere is sleek and modern, the staff professional, and the prices moderate. The 3-course €16 tasting menu at lunch is particularly good value. Reservations highly recommended. Telephone: +39 0648913832. Address: Via del Boschetto 73. *facebook.com/asinodoro*

Li Rioni (Celio/Monti, near the Colosseum)

My old neighborhood pizzeria, this spot is filled with tourists before 8pm… and Italian families after. The pizzas are exactly as Roman pizza should be: crisp, thin, and with fresh, classic ingredients. Telephone: +39 0670450605. Address: Via di SS. Quattro Coronati 24. *lirioni.it*

Monti Bio (Monti, near the Forum)

A great place to stop for a quick lunch or a snack, Monti Bio is a funky little spot with all-local, seasonal goods, like local meats, cheeses, and produce. Grab a soup or a salad to go from the counter, or put together your own *panino* from the fresh offerings. It's located in Monti, the neighborhood near the Colosseum and Roman forum. Telephone: +39 0647824611. Address: Via Panisperna 225.

Osteria Fernanda (Trastevere)

This *osteria* serves up Roman cuisine, with a creative, contemporary twist, for fair prices. And I think it has the best *amatriciana* in Rome. Reservations highly recommended. Telephone: +39 065894333. Address: Via Ettore Rolli 1. *osteriafernanda.com*

Pastificio Guerra (Spanish Steps)

Literally a stone's throw from the Spanish Steps, this pasta shop is a local secret: Every weekday, from 1pm to 2pm, the shop serves "samples" – big, hearty portions of hot, handmade pasta. Along with water and wine, the cost is… €4. Pretty awesome. Telephone: +39 066793102. Address: Via della Croce 8.

Pizzarium (Cipro, near the Vatican museums)

The best pizza you can eat near the Vatican, hands down, is served up at famed pizza chef Gabriele Bonci's Pizzarium. Located right at the Cipro metro station, this foodie haven is renowned for its perfectly chewy dough (thicker than the classic, thin-crust Roman pizzas), high-quality ingredients, and creative concoctions. But it is takeaway, so don't expect a sit-down meal here. Telephone: +39 0639745416. Address: Via della Meloria 43.

Roscioli (Campo dei Fiori)

Known to guidebooks, food bloggers and culinary television shows alike, Roscioli (pronounced row-SHOW-lee) is an institution. It is also every bit as good as all of its evangelists would have you believe. It's not just that the pasta is perfectly cooked or the cured meats melt-in-your-mouth delicious; it's that the ingredients are top-notch and super-fresh. If you think you've had *burrata* before, for example, you haven't had it till you've ordered it here. This isn't a down-home spot for simple cuisine and a cheap bill – while no La Pergola, it's a bit pricier than many of Rome's other traditional spots – but it can be worth the stop. Just keep a close eye on your bill; the last time I was here, I was overcharged. Reservations highly recommended. Telephone: +39 066875287. Address: *Via dei Giubbonari 21. salumeriaroscioli.com*

Urbana 47 (Monti, near the Forum)

Another Monti establishment with an emphasis on local food: All of the ingredients in its dishes are "0km", meaning they come from the Lazio region, and they come directly from their producers. Many ingredients also are certified organic or free-range. In-season dishes have included, in the past, such delicacies as traditional pasta *carbonara*, Roman *stracciatella* or farro, bean and kale soup with pork-rind "salad". Prices are moderate. Telephone: +39 0647884006. Address: Via Urbana 47. *urbana47.it*

Zia Rosetta (Monti, near the Forum)

You may not get a seat at this tiny spot, but if not, don't worry. Take a *panino* away and eat on the little piazza on Via dei Serpenti around the corner. This shop serves up made-to-order sandwiches using fresh ingredients, many of which have an interesting twist (think bresaola with arugula, parmesan, strawberries and balsamic vinegar). They also have smoothies, fresh juices and salads if you want something even lighter. Keep in mind they are open for lunch only from Monday to Thursday, but through to 10pm on Friday to Sunday. Telephone: +39 0631052516. Address: Via Urbana 54. *ziarosetta.com*

Wine and beer

Ai Tre Scalini (Monti, near the Forum)

If you come here in the evening, be prepared to muscle your

way in: This is a local favorite. A traditional *enoteca* with posters and sayings celebrating Monti all over the wall, the small plates here are good (don't miss the fresh *ricotta* with honey), but the real reason to come is for a glass of wine and *taralli*. If you want a table, make sure to book in advance. Telephone: +39 0648907495. Address: Via Panisperna 251. *colosseoorg.wix.com/aitrescalini*

Enoteca Provincia Romana (Forum)

The Provincia di Roma runs this wine bar, so the *enoteca*'s wine and snacks come only from the Rome province (talk about super-local!). As a bonus, it's situated right in the heart of Rome, next to the Imperial Forums and Piazza Venezia. It also serves light meals and snacks. Telephone: +39 0669940273. Address: Via del Foro Traiano 82/84.

Open Baladin (Campo dei Fiori)

You can't get more local than Open Baladin, Rome's #1 hangout for artisanal beers – and which brews its own. Open Baladin's own beers are all-natural, without colorings or preservatives. They've also got some of the best (and only) burgers in Rome. Telephone: +39 066838989. Address: Via degli Specchi 6. *openbaladin.com*

Palatium (Spanish Steps)

As well as a restaurant, Palatium is a wine bar with a long list of Lazio-only wines. Telephone: +39 0669202132. Address: Via Frattina 94.

Il Goccetto (Campo dei Fiori)

This wood-paneled wine bar has a laid-back, old-school feel, down to the frescoes on the ceiling. More than 300 wines hail from Italy and France, and the snacks and nibbles are yummy, too. Telephone: +39 066864268. Address: Via dei Banchi Vecchi 14.

Gelaterias

Carapina (Campo dei Fiori)

Originally from Florence, where it earned a reputation as one of the finest gelaterias in the country, Carapina doesn't make the gelato in Florence and then ship it to Rome (like many others do). Instead, the gelato is made in fresh, small batches right here in the store. There are no preservatives, no synthetic chemicals, and no thickeners. Result: Gelato that bursts with flavor. On a recent visit, I found myself blurting out, just like a kid from a Willy Wonka factory tour, "The persimmon tastes just like persimmon! The chestnut tastes like chestnut!" Which is, of course, how it should be. Address: Via dei Chiavari 37. *carapina.it*

Ciampini (Spanish Steps)

When it comes to gelato, Ciampini, an elegant little cafe on Piazza San Lorenzo in Lucina not far from the Spanish Steps, isn't trendy. The gelato isn't organic. The flavors aren't crazy. The foodies don't (always) flock there. So why do I find I keep coming back for a scoop? It's just. So. Good. The mostly-classic flavors, like pistacchio and coffee, are done as they should be, all high-impact flavor and creamy texture. But what really keeps me returning is the *marron glacés* flavor, where bits of chewy, candied chestnut are mixed in. Pair it with the *cioccolato fondente* (dark chocolate), and it's a match made in gelato heaven. Address: *Piazza San Lorenzo in Lucina 29. ciampini.com*

Come il Latte (Repubblica)

As you might guess from the gelateria's name ("Like Milk"), their gelato comes creamy. Really creamy. That's because fresh cream makes up 40 to 70 percent of each gelato (though some flavors have no milk whatsoever). And from Sicilian pistachios to Ceylon cinnamon, the ingredients are top-notch, fresh, and in season. The caramel with pink Hamalayan salt flavor has become my addiction, while the homemade whipped cream, with flavor choices including *zabaione* (which adds Marsala wine) or *zuppa inglese* (the Italian custard-based dessert), aren't to be missed.

Address: Via Silvio Spaventa, 24/26. *comeillatte.it*

Fior di Luna (Trastevere)

This gelateria, located in the heart of beautiful and popular Trastevere, serves up homemade, artisanal, all-natural gelato. Many of the flavors are made from local ingredients, and the milk is local and organic. Address: Via della Lungaretta 96. *fiordiluna.com*

IL Gelato (Aventine)

The master behind "IL Gelato", Claudio Torcè, is widely revered as the ultimate gelato-maker in Rome. As well as delicious, his gelato is all-natural and homemade. And there are both creative and classic flavors, from hazelnut to chocolate with chili pepper to gorgonzola (yes, the cheese!). Address: Viale Aventino 59, near Circus Maximus. *ilgelatodiclaudiotorce.it*

Gelateria dei Gracchi (Prati, near Castel Sant'Angelo)

After a visit to the Vatican or Castel Sant'Angelo, reward yourself with this homemade gelato made from all-organic, fresh ingredients. I love the chocolate-and-rum (made from fondant, not cocoa powder) and pistachio (made with fresh-roasted Sicilian pistachios) flavors. Address: Via dei Gracchi 272. *gelateriadeigracchi.com*

Gelateria Fatamorgana (Monti and Trastevere)

With fresh ingredients, and *without* colorings, gluten, or chemicals, Fatamorgana's gelato is the real deal. It's also delicious. Check them out at their new location in central Rome, a 10-minute walk from the Forum. Telephone: +39 0686391589. Address: Piazza degli Zingari 5 (Monti) or Via Roma Libera 11 (Trastevere). *gelateriafatamorgana.it*

Gelateria I Caruso (Termini/Repubblica)

At I Caruso, they make their gelato on site (you can even watch them do it!) from all-fresh ingredients. Don't miss their *fondente*, a super-creamy dark chocolate, or the fruit gelatos, which burst with flavor. It's located about a 10-minute walk from the Termini or Repubblica train stations. Address: Via Collina 13/15.

Food markets

La Citta dell'Altra Economia (Testaccio)

In Testaccio, this little "supermarket" is where to find organic, fair-trade foods. The fun part, though, is the farmer's market that *La Citta* hosts. It's only open on occasional Sundays, so check the site before you go. Address: Ex-Mattatoio, Largo Dino Frisullo. *cittadellaltraeconomia.org*

Mercato di Campagna Amica di Circo Massimo (Foro Boario, near Circus Maximus)

Nearly every Saturday and Sunday, Italy's "Campagna Amica" association runs a food market just off Circus Maximus in an easy-to-get-to and lovely part of central Rome. Campagna Amica promotes local, sustainable food – so all of the produce and goods sold here are "0km", meaning from Rome's region of Lazio. As well as fruits and veggies, you can try out cheeses, olive oils, bread, jam, even pastries. If you come around lunchtime, there's often the option to get a sandwich of locally-sourced *porchetta, prosciutto,* or something else, perfect for a meal in the picnic area outside. Address: Via San Teodoro 74. *campagnamica.it*

Mercato Nuovo di Testaccio (Testaccio)

This brand-new space in Testaccio took four years to build, but the result, while somewhat soulless, is also light, airy, and filled with more than 100 local vendors of produce, bread, pastries, jams, and more. It's open every day except Sunday. Address: Via N. Zaglia and Via L. Galvani.

Chapter 7
When in Rome

Shopping

As famous as Rome is for its museums, churches, ruins, and food, there is, of course, something else the city is well-known for: Shopping.

Compared to many other modern cities, Rome has a *lot* of variety when it comes to shopping. The world's most famous high-end designers, from Gucci to Chanel to Louis Vuitton, are all here; so are cheaper chain stores, like Gap, H&M, and Zara.

What makes shopping in Rome really special, though, is that those multinational stores are mixed in with hundreds of independent shops: Individual boutiques, art galleries, "concept stores", and more, that reflect the owner's taste. I love this. It gives such an eclectic flavor to shopping in Rome, and it's something that, I think, is getting completely lost in many other modern cities.

Better yet? Rome's artisans. These men and women take the whole idea of having an independent store one step further, actually making the wares themselves (usually in a workshop right in the back!). The goods you can find handcrafted in Rome run the gamut: Glasswares, leather goods, porcelain, mosaic, clothing, jewelry, housewares, shoes, picture frames, and textiles are just a few.

So when you do your shopping in Rome, I really, really urge you to seek out the independent stores – especially the artisans. Believe it or not, many of them are *not* much more expensive than the High Street shops.

Of course, it can be tough to figure out where to find these places, which are often hole-in-the-wall local secrets. But don't worry – I'm here to help.

In this section, I'll first explain why I've become a fan of independently-run shops, then walk you through shopping in Rome, by neighborhood and share with you a few of my favorite stores.

Why I've turned against chains in Rome

I know that, at least where I come from, almost every clothing store is a chain. So the fact that I harp on about independent stores might seem a little strange.

But just because it's normal back home doesn't mean it's normal in Italy – or that it should be. Italy's tradition is one of independent, family-run stores and artisanal shops. That's what makes shopping in Italy's towns and cities, or even just walking around the streets, so special. You *don't* see the same old thing you do in Every Other City, Anywhere in the World.

Sadly, though, that's changing. More and more small shops, unable to compete with the chains moving in, are having to shut down.

Here, I think, are a few problems with that, aside from the fact that all of these chains are just making Rome boring:

Artisanal traditions are an integral part of Italian culture

And they're dying. But supporting Italy's artisans – ranging from leather workers to mosaicists – helps keep those traditions, and skills, alive.

Plus, it's a great opportunity for the traveler to delve into Italy's culture. Just compare the experience of getting, say, a leather wallet custom-made for you by a Roman artisan versus walking into a Gap and buying a T-shirt.

Multinational retailers take money out of Italy

At least, more than (duh) an independent store does, since labor and materials usually come from abroad. If you want to help the local economy, buy something from an independent or family-run store instead – one that doesn't just have a shopfront here in Italy, but also uses Italian labor, production, and materials. Goodness knows, Italy's economy needs the support!

Factory-made is factory-made

Even at expensive chain stores, I've wound up with bad-quality items that have fallen apart in a matter of days. Although it's nice to think that, at a pricier store, the factories make their goods in a better way, it just doesn't seem to be the case. The best chance you have to ensure that something's top-quality – and that someone has paid real attention to the individual item – is to get it handmade.

The more hands a good passed through on its way to reaching you, the higher the chance that it was touched by crime...

Take this fascinating fact from Roberto Saviano's *Gomorrah:* "The port of Naples handles 20 percent of the value of Italian textile imports from China, but more than 70 percent of the quantity." He continues, "According to the Italian Customs Agency, 60 percent of the goods arriving in Naples escape official customs inspection, 20 percent of the bills of entry go unchecked, and fifty thousand shipments are contraband, 99 percent of them from China – all for an estimated 200 million euros evaded taxes [per four-month period]."

Tax evasion is only a part of it. The illegal trade of

merchandise (and yes, we have *all*, unwittingly, purchased illegal merchandise at some point – even at a legitimate-seeming store) also feeds worldwide crime networks. And we all know how bad those are.

...and the worse it is for the environment...

The more steps a garment had to go through in production and shipping to wind up in your closet, the more likely its trek was *not* so hot for the environment (e.g. thousands of miles of petroleum-heavy shipping and trucking). If we know that local food is better for the environment, why haven't we realized that about local clothing, accessories, and other goods?

...and the likelier it is that human rights were violated.

For clothing at chain stores to be cheap, *very* cheap labor was involved. So it's no wonder that almost every major retailer has wound up in hot water for abuse and child labor: Zara was penalized for the terrible conditions of a factory in Brazil, Forever 21 runs sweatshops both at home and overseas, and Urban Outfitters has been accused of using child labor in Uzbekistan.

Compare it to the local and organic food movement. These days, for example, thoughtful consumers generally accept that you know more about a farm's practices if you know the owners or growers personally. Many people also believe that it's a rare huge, multinational corporation indeed that is more concerned about workers' conditions, food quality, and the health of their product than about the bottom line – and even if the company *does* care, it's pretty difficult for them to have full control over every aspect of their sprawling empire.

The same is true for retail. And when you buy something directly from an artisan, while standing in their workshop in Rome... then you know how the piece was made, and under what conditions. And, for the most part, you can be assured of its quality.

But where in Rome can you find such stores? Just keep reading.

Shopping in the center, by neighborhood

Because there are so many wonderful shops to discover in Rome, it's often easier to simply point people in a certain direction and have them explore on their own than to have a specific list of stores.

Here's what to expect in some of the most popular shopping neighborhoods in the center.

Via del Corso

When you ask someone where to shop in Rome, they usually say this road, which runs from Piazza Venezia to Piazza del Popolo. And that never fails to surprise me.

Once part of the ancient Roman road Via Flaminia, then the thoroughfare where Carnevale horse races took place, Via del Corso is now – in my opinion – in its worst incarnation yet. Rome's "High Street", it's chock-a-block with one chain store after another. H&M. Zara. Athlete's Foot. Another Zara. (Zara, by the way, is now the world's biggest fashion retailer. So even if it seems exotic to us Americans, trust me. There's nothing unique about a Zara store).

Still, this is where *thousands* of people shop. Just go for a walk on Via del Corso on a Friday or Saturday evening and it's shoulder-to-shoulder with both tourists and Italians.

I can never figure it out.

So please… steer clear of shopping here. Here are some other suggestions.

Via Cola di Rienzo

This road, in Prati (near the Vatican), is a good alternative to Via del Corso. There are some good independent stores here, and I tend to return to this area whenever I'm doing shoe shopping, as there are several great shoe stores lining the street.

But there are still way more chains here than I'd like to see. So while this street is a step up from Via del Corso, I prefer one of the four areas I've listed below.

Spanish Steps

The area around the Spanish Steps on up to Piazza del Popolo, including Via del Croce, Via del Babuino, and Via dei Condotti, is a mix of high-end designers (think Gucci, Chanel, Fendi) and some generally-expensive, independent boutiques.

There are a handful of stores here I tend to frequent, but for the most part, the shopping is out of my price range – and, at the end of the day, I prefer to go to neighborhoods in Rome where there are more independently-run shops and artisans. (One exception in this area is Via Margutta, which remains filled with independent art galleries and shops).

Still, it's a fun area to window-shop in, not to mention to watch the elegantly-dressed people.

Piazza Navona and the Pantheon

The cobblestoned back streets around Piazza Navona, including Via Governo Vecchio, Via Dogana Vecchia, and Via dei Coronari, are always fun: Not only are the streets stunning, but their stores vary, including everything from hip furniture stores to musty vintage shops to artisanal jewelers.

In this area, stores tend to be on the high end and generally (although not always) expensive. Still, they're mostly high-quality, independent boutiques and galleries, rather than stores you'd see elsewhere.

Campo dei Fiori

Get off of Campo dei Fiori (contrary to popular belief, the market on the piazza is touristy and anything but authentic, with many stalls now selling made-in-China souvenirs) and onto the back streets around the square, like Via del Pellegrino and Via dei Baullari.

Here's where to find hardworking artisans handcrafting and selling items like picture frames and baskets, right alongside independent clothing boutiques, jewelers, and trendy design stores. In general, these stores are frequented by fewer tourists and the prices are a bit lower than what you'd find in the Piazza Navona, Pantheon, or Spanish Steps areas.

Monti

The neighborhood of Monti, right across from the Forum, is one of my favorite areas for shopping in Rome. There isn't a single chain store (well, except for American Apparel... I'm not sure how they snuck in), and almost all of the artisans here (and there are many!) handcraft and sell goods that are as stylish as they are high-quality and reasonably priced. Here's where to find some of Rome's finest handcrafted fashion, jewelry, glass, mosaic, candles, and more.

Scattered among all of these great artisans are lots of independent boutiques, including a couple of great vintage clothing stores. If you come, make sure to check out Via dei Serpenti, Via del Boschetto, Via Urbana, and Via Panisperna. And on (most) Sundays, Mercato Monti takes place, showcasing local designers and sellers of vintage items.

Just a few of my favorite shops

Don't let the chain stores on Via del Corso fool you: Rome still has a number of unique, independent boutiques and artisans. I couldn't possibly list them all, but these are just some of the places where I like to do my shopping.

Please note again that many of Rome's best stores, including artisanal shops and boutiques, close at about 12pm or 1pm. They then reopen around 4pm, and remain open until about 8pm. Many also close on Sundays and Mondays through lunchtime. So plan your spree accordingly.

Armando Rioda (leather bags & accessories; Spanish Steps and Piazza Navona)

Since 1949, this workshop has been turning out handcrafted

leather wallets, purses, luggage and jackets. There are only a few items on-the-rack, so what Armando Rioda shines in is the custom-made item. For just €50, you can pick the leather, color and style of, say, a leather passport holder, and have it monogrammed, too. Purses start at €100, which is still a steal for having a handmade leather bag. Because the owners have parted ways, there now are two locations, each with a different name. (Given their shared history, I'm listing both here as a single item). One, now called **Pelletteria Nives,** is at Via delle Carrozze 16, on the second floor, near the Spanish Steps; ring number 6 on the bell. (It's worth calling Nives at +39 3385370233 or Vinicio at +39 3333370831 to double-check their hours before stopping by). The other location, called **Rioda 1950**, is at Via del Cancello 14/15, just north of Piazza Navona; call them at +39 066784942 or email them at rioda1950@gmail.com.

Ashanti Galleria (jewelry; Monti)

In the 12 years that jeweler Raffaelle Cinzio has been running this jewelry/art space, he's received serious accolades, like a mark of excellence for artisanship from the region of Lazio. Not that it's any surprise: Raffaelle's jewelry, handcrafted from silver, bronze, and gold in his workspace at the back of Ashanti Galleria, manages to be both exquisite and funky, much of it with a cool, androgynous tone. Contemporary paintings by artists, most of them Italian, hang on the walls. Sound too upmarket for your wallet? Actually, Raffaelle's jewelry starts at €45 a pop, and the works of art at €100. Telephone: +39 064884203. Address: Via del Boschetto 117. *ashantigalleria.com*

Barrila' Boutique (women's shoes; Spanish Steps)

Established in 1954, this shop near the Spanish Steps sells handmade suede and leather women's shoes, including ballet flats, wedges, and pumps. Every style comes in a range of colors. Prices are reasonable, especially for the area; expect to pay about €50 and up for a pair of shoes. Telephone: +39 063245046. Address: Via del Babuino 33a. *barrilaboutique.it*

Bohemienne (men's and women's vintage clothes; Campo dei Fiori)

This store near Campo dei Fiori has a small but well-edited collection of vintage clothes and accessories, from men's tweed jackets to elegant blouses. Telephone: +39 0668804011. Address: Via dei Cappellari 96. *facebook.com/BohemienneRoma*

Eclectica (knickknacks and curiosities; Pantheon)

Even looking in the window of Eclectica is a bizarre treat. (Which is lucky, since the prices make it out of reach for most people). Like something out of a Roman version of Harry Potter, this store sells everything from magic wands to tarot cards (it's the oldest magic store in Italy), but also a number of collectibles, from antique toys to military souvenirs. Eclectic indeed. Telephone: +39 066784228. Address: Via in Aquiro 70. *eclecticamagic.com*

Le Nou (women's clothes)

This is the kind of hole-in-the-wall you could easily pass by. Don't! The hip folks behind Le Nou design, and then hand-sew, trendy creations right there in the store lab. If something you like is hanging on the rack, they can alter the size for your right there; if you want something from scratch, they can turn it around within 24 hours. Lest you think such top-notch service means "expensive," just wait: Blouses start at €30. Yep, you heard me. The same price as at Zara. Telephone: +39 0631056339. Email: lenou@hotmail.it. Address: Via del Boschetto 111.

LoL (women's clothes; Monti)

Although the prices of this trendy boutique in Monti might seem high, the products are each unique and handmade by Italian artisans. There's an "alternative" line made out of all organic materials, too. Telephone: +39 064814160. Address: Via Urbana 89. *lolroma.com*

King Size Vintage (men's and women's vintage clothes;

Monti)

This store features big, but well-edited, collections of everything to outfit a fashion maven's vintage wardrobe, from shoes to belts, bags to jackets. Prices are typical for a Rome vintage store – about €35 or so for a blouse. Address: Via Leonina 78/79. Telephone: +39 064817045. *facebook.com/kingsize.vintage*

Kokoro (women's clothes; Monti)

Items at this "clothing laboratory" are up-to-the-minute (items change weekly) and frankly fabulous, with lots of play with color, prints, and texture (hello, suede leggings!). All the items, which include purses and accessories, are original creations. Blouses are about €40, dresses €70. Telephone: +39 0664760251. Address: Via del Boschetto 75. *kokoroshop.it*

La Bottega del Marmoraro (marble engraving; Spanish Steps)

In this little workshop near the Spanish Steps, the owner, Sandro, continues his father's tradition by etching and carving marble pieces. What better idea for a gift than a €15 piece, engraved with a saying? Telephone: +39 063207660. Address: Via Margutta 53b.

Mancini (leather; Pantheon)

The little shop, tucked behind the Pantheon, got its start back in 1918. The great-grandson of the first owner runs it today. For a small place, it's had an illustrious history: It provided leather for the 1951 film Quo Vadis, once made a leather folder (random, yes) for Pope Pius XII and was Gucci's go-to spot for repairs for years. The goods here are still handcrafted (hardly a given in today's Rome). The style of the bags, belts and wallets here veer toward a traditional, classic style, though they often employ fun colors. In terms of prices, you're looking at a small leather bag for around €200, a leather tote for around €250 and briefcases around €300. Address: Via della Palombella 28. *mancinileather.it*

Maurizio Grossi (marble and mosaic; Spanish Steps)
Located near the Spanish Steps on Via Margutta, Rome's most atmospheric and art-filled street (Picasso even had his studio here), Maurizio Grossi's gallery features every marble and mosaic item imaginable – including statue reproductions, bookends, inlaid marble tables, even succulent-looking (marble) fruits. Telephone: +39 0636001935. Address: Via Margutta 109. *mauriziogrossi.com*

Mercato Monti (clothes, jewelry and accessories; Monti)
Taking place most weekends in Monti (check the website for upcoming dates), this little market of carefully-chosen vendors gets crowded with fashionistas and in-the-know locals. Vendors sell everything from vintage sunglasses to handmade bracelets to imported frocks, and it's the perfect place to find gifts (including for yourself!). Just check the website to make sure it's on. Address: Via Leonina 46. *mercatomonti.com*

Picta Porcellane (porcelain; Campo dei Fiori)
Just around the corner from Campo dei Fiori, this little studio is where Marina Graziana handpaints porcelain cups, bowls, saucers, and more; styles range from whimsical to elegant. Prices, starting at €15 for a small plate, are reasonable. Telephone: +39 0668300248. Address: Via dei Cappellari 11. *pictaporcellane.com*

Pulp (women's vintage clothes; Monti)
The owner of this cult favorite in Monti takes vintage clothes and updates them with a creative, modern twist (although some items are sold as-is). Prices are good; I've bought belts here for €15 and blouses for €25. Telephone: +39 06485511. Address: Via del Boschetto 140.

Studio Silice (glass; Monti)
At this small workshop in Monti, glass artisan Anna Preziosi handcrafts gorgeous, light-catching plates, vases, decorations, and more. Prices start at €15 for an ashtray or small dish, and yes, she can pack your baubles securely if you're worried about

transporting them back home. Telephone: +39 064745552. Email: studiosilice@gmail.com. Address: Via Urbana 27. *studiosilice.com*

Tina Sondergaard (women's clothes; Monti)
The clothes at this tiny shop in Monti, all designed by English-speaking Danish import Sondergaard, are hand-stitched and top-quality. The fabrics come from just outside Florence. Along with her whimsical but classy pieces, Sondergaard will create items by request – she's made everything from costumes to wedding dresses in the past. But even her bespoke work won't break the bank: She's even custom-made a cocktail dress for €200. Telephone: +39 3343850799. Address: Via del Boschetto 1d. *facebook.com/ Tina.Sondergaard.Rome/*

Twice (men's and women's vintage clothes; Trastevere)
A vintage shop that's anything but musty, Twice, in the heart of Trastevere, has a gorgeous collection of clothes, shoes and accessories, mainly from the 1960s to 1980s. I found a pristine, vintage Chanel purse here once for €250. I still regret not buying it. Telephone: +39 065816859. Email: sisterstwice@gmail.com. Address: Via di San Francesco a Ripa 7. *twicevintage.com*

A final note

I hope you've enjoyed this handbook to exploring, and enjoying, Rome like a local.

Don't forget that if you have any other questions, you have several more resources at your fingertips. There's a good deal of more information on my blog, revealedrome.com. You also can follow Revealed Rome on Facebook, Twitter and Instagram.

If you want to be able to *really* pick my brain about travel to Italy, you can book a one-on-one travel chat with me. From recommending specific hotels in your price range to helping you plan your itinerary, my personalized advice can help make your trip truly special. Here is just some recent feedback from clients:

"All of your recommendations were perfect! This was my 3rd visit to Rome and I naively thought to myself that I had "done" and seen most of Rome. All your recommendations proved that I have so much more to see and experience… And thank you for the recommendation on stopping by in Narni, Todi and Gubbio. Each little town was so charming and such a treat to explore on our own." *–Kristine Fletcher, Washington, D.C., trip to Rome, Tuscany and Umbria*

"Amanda's one-hour consulting sessions are bookended by an email exchange to set needs and expectations, and a follow up that includes her incredibly practical guide to seeing the sights, eating, and shopping in the Eternal City. Worth every penny. We never would have discovered gems like Pastificio or Open Baladin without having connected with Amanda." *–Steve McIntosh, Columbus, Ohio, trip to Rome*

"Thanks again for the consultation. It made all the difference for us. Whenever we were thinking outside of the box, we'd remind ourselves, 'What did Mandy say about this?'" *–Peter Graves, Phoenix, Arizona, trip to Rome and Venice*

"We loved all of your suggestions… I can't thank you enough! We're already discussing our next trip." *–Rachel Sussman, New York, N.Y., trip to Sicily and Rome*

Other reasons to consider chatting with me, rather than depending on a guidebook or a travel agent:

- **I know Italy** backwards, forwards, and upside-down. Over the last few years, I've traveled several times to *each* of the following places in Italy: Florence, Venice, Verona, Naples, Pompeii, the Amalfi coast, Sicily, Tuscany beyond Florence (Lucca, Pisa, Siena, and more), Puglia, Umbria (Assisi, Orvieto, Bevagna and more), Emilia-Romagna, Cinque Terre, and Matera. I lived in the Italian Alps for two months, too.

- **I lived in Rome** for more than four years. Even the best travel agents or travel writers usually have only been visitors. I was a local – which means I was able to really gather the insider's tips and knowledge I wouldn't have if I'd just been there on vacation. Now based in London, I still travel to Rome at least a couple of times a year.

- **My articles** on Italy have been published in a variety of publications, including National Geographic Traveller, New York Times, Travel + Leisure, BBC and the Guardian. I've also contributed to seven different Fodor's guidebooks.

- **I don't take commissions.** From anyone. So if I recommend a restaurant, hotel, or whatever else, you can rest assured it's because I genuinely think you'd love it; there's no kickback to me whatsoever.

Want to know more? Email me at revealedrome@gmail.com or book your session at revealedrome.com/italy-travel-consulting.

Thanks again for listening to my tips and tricks, and enjoy your time in the Eternal City!

76726848R00132

Made in the USA
San Bernardino, CA
15 May 2018